A Clinician's Guide to Compassion Focused Group Therapy for the Severely Mentally Ill

This manual provides clinicians with guidance to conduct compassion focused group therapy with patients suffering from severe forms of mental illness.

Historically, those suffering from severe forms of mental illness face a myriad of biological, psychological, and social challenges, particularly shame and self-criticism. Compassion focused therapy is known to combat and address this suffering. This manual connects rich biological, psychological, and social theory with empirical findings and lived clinical experience. Comprising 12 modules, this clinician's guide presents psychoeducation in conjunction with intrapersonal/interpersonal exercises and process-oriented instructions to aid treatment and guide group therapy sessions.

This book, created by clinicians for clinicians, is a vital resource for psychiatrists, psychologists, social workers, or substance use disorder counselors, offering compassion focused group therapy in an inpatient setting.

Aileen Rands, MS, is a doctoral candidate with over five years of working with SMI individuals. She is currently completing her pre-doctoral internship at Veteran Affairs Administration. She is an emerging psychologist with an interest in severe psychopathology and group psychotherapy.

Doug Benson, PsyD, DBT-LBC, is a psychologist with 20 years of experience working with SMI. He is board-certified in DBT, is a clinical supervisor for Utah State Hospitals psychology internship/postdoc, develops treatment programing, participates in clinical research in conjunction with Brigham Young University, and provides clinical services.

Amanda L. Rapacz, PsyD, has worked for the State of Utah in the Department of Health and Human Services at Utah State Hospital since 2009 and is currently the assistant superintendent. She is the licensed psychologist serving on the State of Utah's Division of Professional Licensing Behavioral Health Board. Her passion for the field of psychology and working with individuals who have severe and persistent mental illness has led to presidential positions on the Utah Psychological Association and NAMI-Utah boards.

Gary Burlingame, PhD, has 40+ years of training, teaching, and research experience on effective group therapies, recognized by US and international professional associations. He began focusing on outpatient SMI treatment in the 1990s, with 25 years of service developing inpatient group programming. He was the president of the American Group Psychotherapy Association and the Society of Group Psychology and Group Psychotherapy.

A Clinician's Guide to Compassion Focused Group Therapy for the Severely Mentally Ill

Aileen Rands, Doug Benson,
Amanda L. Rapacz, and Gary Burlingame

Routledge
Taylor & Francis Group
NEW YORK AND LONDON

Designed cover image: © Getty Images

First published 2026
by Routledge
605 Third Avenue, New York, NY 10158

and by Routledge
4 Park Square, Milton Park, Abingdon, Oxon, OX14 4RN

Routledge is an imprint of the Taylor & Francis Group, an informa business

ISBN: 978-1-003-86388-5 (hbk)
ISBN: 978-1-003-86387-8 (pbk)
ISBN: 978-1-003-60755-7 (ebk)

DOI: 10.4324/9781003607557

Typeset in Sabon
by Apex CoVantage, LLC

Contents

About the Manual

Compassion focused therapy (CFT) is a therapeutic modality aimed at understanding, alleviating, and preventing suffering in oneself and others (Gilbert, 2009). CFT specifically aids those suffering from shame and self-criticism. Historically, those with severe forms of mental illness have been subject to marginalization and stigmatization resulting in enduring shame and/or self-criticism. This trend can still be seen today in those struggling with chronic and complicated psychopathology. *A Clinician's Guide to Compassion Focused Group Therapy for the Severely Mentally Ill* is a 12-module manual for conducting CFT group therapy for those struggling with serious or severe mental illness (SMI). The stigma that accompanies this population carries even into the terminology used to classify those within this umbrella. The terminology of "SMI" has risen in popularity within psychology in both academic and clinical spaces, as mental healthcare differs substantially from those with more "moderate" to "mild" mental illness. SMI commonly refers to mental illness conditions that result in serious functional impairment of which substantially effects quality of life. SMI often includes but is not limited to schizophrenia (and associated disorders), bipolar disorders, and persistent depressive disorders. The vast majority of individuals with SMI presentations experience complex comorbidities. Ultimately, we hope that those who use this manual understand the unique challenges this population face while recognizing how vast this group can be.

Growing research supports CFT's effectiveness in treating clinical populations (Millard et al., 2023). In terms of SMI, research suggests that CFT is a feasible and promising treatment for transdiagnostic groups comprised of those with acute psychiatric conditions. For example, CFT has been found to increase compassion, decrease depression, and decrease social marginalization for those with schizophrenia-spectrum disorders (Braehler et al., 2013a). Further, CFT delivered in inpatient settings to those with SMI has been found to decreased distress, increased calmness, improve understanding of compassion, increase positive affect, and connection with the experience of common humanity (Heriot-Maitland et al., 2014). By treating underlying psychological processes rather than symptoms alone, CFT has the potential to treat shame and self-criticism in transdiagnostic group settings (Cuppage et al., 2018). It is clear that CFT principles and material is empirically supported. Thus far, study of CFT in SMI settings has entailed adoption of ideas and interventions found within original CFT material, given the unique needs and challenges of those with SMI. Despite site-by-site adaptation and growing study, no manual exists for CFT delivery to those with SMI in group format. This manual addresses this need.

This manual was tailored from prior CFT material to specifically fit the SMI population and to be delivered in a group format. It was tailored by expert clinicians, all of whom have direct experience providing CFT to SMI individual within an inpatient state hospital setting. Edits were informed by years of this clinical experience as well as research efforts. Each module in this manual presents psychoeducation interventions in conjunction with intrapersonal/interpersonal exercises, and process-oriented instructions. CFT principles are taught according to situations/experiences/scenarios brought to the CFT group space by SMI individuals. Module content can always be adapted according to the needs of the group and setting. This manual is designed to be used by any licensed mental health clinicians typically found with an inpatient setting (e.g., psychiatrists [MD], clinical psychologists [PhD, PsyD], social workers [MS], substance use disorder counselors [SUDC], etc.). The manual should be used in conjunction with the manual's companion *Compassion Focused Therapy for SMI Participant Workbook*. This workbook provides patients with summaries of session content, handouts, and key exercises to practice outside of session.

Key Contributions

In addition to the primary editors/authors, key contributions were also made by Ben Roos, PsyD; Patty Weaver, LCSW; Rachel Arnold, PhD; Tate Paxton, MS; and Gabriel Hoose, BS.

This manual was made possible with the generous support of Professor Paul Gilbert and Drs. James Kirby and Nicola Petrocchi, who made available their manual on compassion focused therapy from which we have adapted this work. Further, we are grateful for the efforts of Kara Cattani, Derek Griner, David Erikson, Gary Burlingame Mark Beecher, and Cameron Alldredge (2021), whose *CFT Manual for University Counseling Centers* also informed this work. Last, this manual was made possible by the pioneering contributions of Dr. Charlie Heriot-Maitland who has applied and studied CFT treatment for SMI conditions, specifically those involving psychosis.

List of Illustrations

Handouts

Figures

Foreword

While the cultivation of compassion has been recommended for thousands of years as a way to support mental well-being and positive social relationships, it has only been in the last 30 years or so that we began to understand the process involved in compassion motivation and action. Today, we have many studies showing key physiological changes in brain and body when people stimulate compassion motivation (Singer, 2025). The question has always been *how* to harness and cultivate these brain states, for people in general but also for people with mental health difficulties, and indeed, there are a number of different approaches with some evidence of effectiveness (Kirby et al., 2017). My approach to mental health problems has always been rooted in understanding the underlying evolved functions and processes and their psychosocial manifestations in brain states (Gilbert 1989 1995 Gilbert & Simos, 2022). Compassion focused therapy (CFT), therefore, grew out of this way of conceptualizing mental processes, but it was also linked to standard, evidence-based interventions. Crucially, however, it developed for and with individuals who often came from traumatic backgrounds, had not responded particularly well to standard therapies, and had chronic or more complex difficulties. As of today, for both the severe and less severe clients, there is increasing evidence of effectiveness of CFT. In a recent study of 47 controlled trials from the last 14 years, with data from 7,875 participants from 17 countries, CFT was effective in reducing overall negative mental health outcomes ($k = 32$, $g = 0.72$, $p < .0001$), depression ($k = 23$, $g = 0.49$, $p < .0001$), self-criticism ($k = 17$, $g = 0.40$, $p < .0001$) and in improving compassion for self and others ($k = 24$, $g = 0.51$, $p < .0001$) (Petrocchi et al., 2024). In regard to people experiencing the more severe end of the spectrum, there are fewer studies, but these show very promising results (see Braehler et al., 2013; Gilbert et al., 2022; Heriot-Maitland, 2024; Heriot-Maitland & Longden, 2022; Heriot-Maitland et al., 2023; Mayhew & Gilbert, 2008). Clearly, more research is needed.

CFT is called compassion *focused* therapy, *not* compassion therapy, because it's a way of contextualizing multiple interventions from across a number of therapeutic domains but engaging them with activation of the biological, psychological, and social processes of compassion. As part of that, we indicate how these processes are evolved with functions. We can then help clients recognize that our dispositions for anxiety, depression, paranoia, and so forth are not our fault because they are part of our brain's potentials that get shaped, for better or worse, by life experiences. After all, no one wakes up in the morning and deliberately chooses to have a depression or panic attack or to hear frightening voices; these come against our will. We can, however, choose to do positive things, such as plan a holiday with friends or cooking a nice meal. So on the whole, the stressed states of mind are not chosen, whereas positive states of mind can be (if contexts allow). This provides a platform for depersonalization, decentering, de-shaming and as a way to become a mindful observer of what we call tricky brain.

Crucially, then, a CFT therapist has to be familiar with a range of different processes not only on therapy in general, such as how to run groups, but also on the process underpinning different dimensions of compassion and their delivery within the therapy. They can distinguish between the therapeutic processes, be it with individuals or groups, and what we call *compassionate mind training*. These are specific practices designed to cultivate different elements of the compassion motivational system and can be taught in the standalone self-help way outside a specific therapy. Helping clients practice mind training exercises can be quite a challenge.

This book is notable for a number of reasons. First, it was the basis for Aileen's PhD under the guidance of Professor Gary Burlingame, an internationally recognized group psychotherapist who, in 2015, came to Derby and spent time with us learning about CFT. I was developing a group manual at the time, and we were able to share that together. He and his colleagues went on to develop it and apply it to student health problems (Fox et al., 2021). Doug and Amanada bring their many years of experience in working with people with severe mental health difficulties. So they all had a combination of talents.

The book itself is laid out as therapies tend to be laid out as a series of expanding experiential and educational modules. Helping clients develop frameworks to understand the nature of their experiences in non-shaming and non-blaming ways, and to hold such experiences with compassion rather than fear shame rage, set the stage for therapists and clients to construct new meaning and texture to the experience. This enables clients to have new insights into how and why mindfulness can be so important. They are learning what they are mindful of—the operations of a very tricky brain they never chose. This is part of that more detailed information about how the motives and emotions work in our brains. People can come to understand that we are all "designed" for survival and reproduction that gives rise to three functions. All living things have to be able to detect threats and take some kind of defensive action to protect their survival. All living things need to also be able to find and utilize resources that facilitate survival and flourishing and the ability to secure major life tasks and biosocial goals. This includes, of course, finding food to eat and shelter, securing mating opportunities and sexually reproducing, and subsequently caring for offspring. A third task is the ability to rest and digest when not under threat, not needing to focus on defensive actions and not being in states of having to seek and strive to meet needs or obtain resources. This is called *rest and digest*, which has its own physiological profile. It has fundamental impacts on physiological processes and balancing threat and drive.

Module 2 explores what is called *the three emotion regulation* systems, where we can identify emotions linked to threat sensitivities, such as anger, anxiety, and disgust; emotions linked to reward and resource seeking and striving *towards* biosocial goals, such energizing, pleasure, and excitement when achieved; and emotions linked to settling the body and mind for "rest and digest." The *balance and co-regulation and context-appropriate functioning* of these three motive-emotion systems are key to mental well-being, but in people who struggle with mental states, it can be highly dysregulated. For some people, especially when threat processes dominate, as is not uncommon for individuals who have trauma, they can cause much suffering. Ways in which compassion motivation can bring balance to these systems is very important.

Module 3 brings these two themes together such that clients can learn how to be mindful and how to open attention to the fluctuating activations of these different systems within us. We can begin to notice that "this is anger arising from my anger system" or "this is anxiety arising." There is now good evidence that the ability to be mindful and label our experience can be very helpful rather than being lost in them and particularly if we can do that with a compassionate texture of recognizing this is not our fault that we are experiencing the impact activations of evolved biological systems in certain contexts.

Safeness, which is distinct from safety (Gilbert, 2024), is therefore very important because safety is monitored by the threat system as to whether threats exist or don't, whereas safeness is monitored by the availability of *positive resources*, particularly the helpfulness of others, and the pleasures of affiliative relating. Imagine, for example, being with people who you know care about you and will help you if you need them to (in contrast to people or strangers who are indifferent or maybe even critical if you have states of emotional need and vulnerability). Safeness evolved within the "rest and digest" system because it has a settling and calming impact on threat and striving—which what are the effects of caring. However, caring is not only soothing, but as in attachment theory, it also provides a secure base that enables us to take the courage to go out explore and try things and this is very important in group therapy—that it should provide both the soothing but also secure base, encouraging risk taking and engaging behaviors. The social dynamic of social safeness is highlighted in Module 4. It is a very important focus because it is to help clients experienced the group as safe in the sense that they experience others as being mutually supportive with a caring interest in each other. Indeed, the sense of common humanity and empathy with concern for each other is one of the most important dynamics of group therapy. Social safeness is linked to our abilities to experience compassion from others in supportive ways, being self-compassionate, and also having an interest in being compassionate to others, which is the subject of Module 4.

In CFT, one is always helping class think about how they are relating to the external world come at their ability to be mindful empathic and caring but also have their relating to their own internal worlds. Here, the focus is on understanding the nature of self-identity and organizing one's mind and practices around the core values of compassion. In Buddhist approaches, this is called *bodhicitta*. Crucial here is to explore with people their fears, blocks, and resistances. These can be linked to many things, such as lack of clarity about the nature of compassion and confusion with niceness or kindness as opposed to courage and wisdom. Kindness is a way of being compassion, but it is not compassion itself. Resistances can also arise from unprocessed problems, such as rage, and it can be because we need to break down the skills of compassion into the doable.

Module 6 highlights the fact that CFT is highly focused on the issue of co-regulation of processes; for example, the way we regulate each other in our relationships and communications. However, we know that we can relate to ourselves in fairly similar ways that we relate to others. In other words, we can be angry with ourselves, or anxious with ourselves, or happy or satisfied, and so on. This is because we are utilizing what is called social mentalities, which are specialist processing systems designed to process different types of social relationship. This means we can have multiple systems firing off at the same time. For example, if we have an argument with somebody we care about, there may be a part of us as feeling angry, but another part may be anxious about the dispute or anxious about not letting our anger be damaging to the relationship or feeling sad over the rupture in the relationship or even happy that this may well resolve some difficulties for long-term benefit. For people with mental health difficulties, these complexities and conflicts with different priorities in the mind can be highly dysregulating. Therefore, helping clients begin to mindfully recognize not only the nature of the *multiple potentials* within them (the multiplicity of mind) but also how those multiple potentials relate and co-regulate each other. Again activating the compassion motivational system enables the client to bring harmony because they can become compassionate to their angry, anxious, or sad brain system, as well as focus on how they would like the argument to resolve.

Module 7 addresses the issue of hostile self-relating in the form of self-criticism. Self-criticism itself can, of course, be helpful because it's simply an awareness that one has behaved in a way against one's intentions or has made a mistake or can learn how to do better. Provided the emotional textures are ones of compassion and support that is usually encouraging. It becomes problematic, however, when it's driven by disappointment and fear and then it becomes hostile and attacking. It is the hostile and attacking that is self-judgement because it's been generated by stimulating by threat processing. This is why we always explore the emotional textures of the criticism, not just the content. Compassion is not about not taking responsibility for problematic behavior but rather understanding it in a way that's non-defensive such that we are genuinely able to encourage support and understand ourselves to make changes.

Clients with severe mental health problems can be burdened with extensive shame as explored in Module 8. There are a number of different forms of shame. External shame is the shame we can feel when we experience other people are looking down on us or being critical or rejecting us in some way. Internal shame is when we are hostile *to ourselves*, as in hostile self-criticism. Many people avoid seeking help or avoid revealing the nature of their mental health difficulty because of their fear of others' response. Hence, group therapy can be ideal for addressing external shame through processes of common humanity and how the therapist helps clients feel safe in opening up about things they're ashamed about. Distinguishing guilt and shame is very important in CFT because, unlike cognitive therapy, CFT grounds these in very different motivational systems and therefore has quite different therapeutic interventions.

As the modules unfold, it becomes clearer that compassion is really about developing the *courage and wisdom* to interact with our very tricky potentially harmful brain and at times tricky relationships. In addition, clients can sometimes recognize they can begin to take on compassion motivation as a way of living, not just as a way of dealing with difficult symptoms and experiences.

In the last three modules, the authors really focus on bringing compassion into everyday life and in particular into social relationships. With Module 10 we enter the important world of assertiveness because compassion can sometimes be confused with niceness and kindness, which are quite different. Here, the therapists make this clear all the way through. In many ways, comparison focused assertiveness follows relatively straightforward standard assertive training, which involves clarity of message and validation of self and other, with respect for the other rather than attacking. Indeed, one of the problems that clients sometimes have with anger is they fuse it with aggression and are not clear how to have forms of respectful non-attacking but firm assertiveness.

Module 11 focuses on forgiveness, which can be extremely difficult for some clients, particularly those who have come from very abusive or hurtful backgrounds. As these therapists make clear forgiveness work cannot be undertaken unless clients have insight into the value of forgiveness and are motivated which they won't be if they haven't addressed their underlying pain and rage. Helping clients understand that forgiveness is really about dealing with one's own a rage and vengeance, not condoning what was done, can be essential. As the therapists make clear, you may never like or want to see the person you're forgiving. On the other side of forgiveness is apology, which is sometimes forgotten. But we also need to learn to be sincere in our apologies. If we ourselves have done things that are harmful or hurtful to others, then apologies are not submissive or giving in but are respectful. In CFT, then we have the three dynamics of assertiveness forgiveness and apology

Module 12 offers ways in which clients can reflect together on their journey, explore the processes of change they have gone through, including their courage and wisdom they brought to their therapy sessions, and begin to think about how they'd like to begin to live from their compassionate motivational system. It is important to help people recognize that we can't necessarily change the weather, but we can change how we work with it. In other words, we may still be vulnerable to the comings and goings of problematic mental states, but if we can stay mindful as best as we can and hold the storms of the mind with a compassionate frame, this can help. So this session can be an opportunity for clients to start to predict the potential for triggers to arise and how they can practice what they're going to do in the future. They can also practice not just being responsive to troublesome mental states but also changes they may like to make in their life in terms of positive movement forward in order to flourish and build self-confidence.

This book is not written as a clear moment-by-moment text, with details about processes and very comprehensive references, but it seeks to provide a set of guides and ideas for you in your group work with CFT. It is full of diagrams and worksheets that you can use directly or adapt, ways of explaining things to clients, and ways of offering stories and reflections. Different groups in different populations require different textures to therapy, so it's important to be flexible and open while following some of the core processes of CFT. CFT is a way of thinking about the nature of how and why our minds evolved in the way they have and with all kinds of complexities to them. Compassion can harmonize some of the storms that go on in them. I'm sure this book will help you develop your compassion approaches used in working with the distressed states of mind that you will encounter in our therapeutic work.

Professor Paul Gilbert, OBE
Author of *The Compassionate Mind* (2009) and
Compassion Focused Therapy (2010)
President of the Compassionate Mind Foundation

References

Braehler, C., Gumley, A., Harper, J., Wallace, S., Norrie, J., & Gilbert, P. (2013). Exploring change processes in compassion focused therapy in psychosis: Results of a feasibility randomized controlled trial. British Journal of Clinical Psychology, 52, 199–214.

Fox, J., Cattani, K., & Burlingame, G. M. (2021). Compassion focused therapy in a university counseling and psychological services center: A feasibility trial of a new standardized group manual. Psychotherapy Research, 31(4), 419–431.

Gilbert, P. (2024). Threat, safety, safeness and social safeness 30 years on: Fundamental dimensions and distinctions for mental health and well-being. British Journal of Clinical Psychology, 63, 453–471.

Gilbert, P., Basran, J., Minou, L., Rayner, A., Hayes, A., Lucre, K., McEwan, K., Byrne, F., & Newton, L. (2022). Compassion Focused Group Therapy for people with a diagnosis of bipolar affective disorder: A feasibility study. Frontiers in Psychology, 13, 841932. https://doi.org/10.3389/fpsyg.2022.841932.

Heriot-Maitland, C. (2024). Position paper–CFT for psychosis. Psychology and Psychotherapy: Theory, Research and Practice, 97(1), 59–73.

Heriot-Maitland, C., Gumley, A., Wykes, T., Longden, E., Irons, C., Gilbert, P., & Peters, E. (2023). A case series study of compassion-focused therapy for distressing experiences in psychosis. The British Journal of Clinical Psychology. https://doi.org/10.1111/bjc.12437.

Heriot-Maitland, C., & Longden, E. (2022). Relating to Voices Using Compassion Focused Therapy: A Self-Help Companion. Routledge.

Mayhew, S., & Gilbert, P. (2008). Compassionate mind training with people who hear malevolent voices: A case series report. Clinical Psychology and Psychotherapy, 15, 113–138.

Petrocchi, N., Ottaviani, C., Cheli, S., Matos, M., Baldi, B., Basran, J. K., & Gilbert, P. (2024). The Impact of Compassion-Focused Therapy on positive and negative mental health outcomes: Results of a series of meta-analyses. Clinical Psychology: Science and Practice, 31, 230–247. https://dx.doi.org/10.1037/cps0000193.

Singer, T. (2025). A neuroscience perspective on the plasticity of the social and relational brain. Annals of the New York Academy of Sciences, 1547(1), 52–74.

Acknowledgments

We begin with our ongoing gratitude to Dr. Paul Gilbert, who generously shared his CFT work with members of our team. His passion for and genius in aiding those who suffer deeply from the burden of mental illness inspired and propelled our work. He first welcomed Dr. Burlingame into the circle of friends and colleagues who support his work in the United Kingdom and later embraced more at Brigham Young University (BYU). This association and collaboration became instrumental in the introduction and integration of CFT at the Utah State Hospital (USH), of which houses the most severely mentally ill individuals from across the state. We deeply appreciate the support of Professor Paul Gilbert and Drs. James Kirby and Nicola Petrocchi, who made available their manual on compassion focused therapy from which we have adapted this work. Additionally, this manual would not be possible without the work and consultation of many members of the Compassionate Mind Foundation scattered throughout the world. We are particularly grateful to Charlie Heriot-Maitland and Eleanor Longden in their application of CFT for those who experience voice hearing, as widely common experience within the SMI population. Their writing, research, and insight incredibly supplements this manual. Finally, we would also like to acknowledge the work of Kara Cattani, Derek Griner, David Erekson, Gary Burlingame Mark Beecher, and Cameron Alldredge (2021) in their work on the counseling center adaptation of CFT, a team of clinicians whose hard work paved the way for the creation of this manual. We would also like to thank the many students, patients, and clinicians involved in research contributing to the evidence of CFT's feasibility and effectiveness for those with SMI. We appreciate all those who acknowledge that the most difficult of patient are often the ones who need compassion the most.

Several authors contributed equally and in different ways to the adaptation of this manual.

Introduction

To start, we recommend you should have a firm theoretical and clinical understanding of small group treatment. The American Psychological Association's Group Psychology and Group Psychotherapy specialty describes the skills needed to run a small group (see https://www.apa.org/ed/graduate/specialize/group-psychology-therapy).

Second, prior to providing any CFT interventions, clinicians should (1) have a firm understanding of the integrative science and practice of CFT and (2) engage in their own practice of mindful compassion. To better understand the science and practice, we recommend the following reading:

Articles

Gilbert, P. (2009). "Introducing compassion-focused therapy." *Advances in Psychiatric Treatment*, 15(3), 199–208.https://doi.org/10.1192/apt.bp.107.005264

Gilbert, P. (2017). "A brief outline of the evolutionary approach for compassion focused therapy." *EC Psychology and Psychiatry*, 3(6), 218–227.

Gilbert, P. (2019). "Psychotherapy for the 21st century: An integrative, evolutionary, contextual, biopsychosocial approach." *Psychology and Psychotherapy: Theory, Research and Practice*, 92(2), 164–189.

Books and Book Chapters

The following book is recommended in full. Certain chapters are listed to guide clinicians in learning more about how CFT might apply to individuals with certain diagnostic presentations typically experienced by those with SMI.

Gilbert, P. & Simos, G. (2022). *Compassion Focused Therapy: Clinical Practice and Applications*. Routledge. https://doi.org/10.4324/9781003035879

Personality Disorders

Chapter 16: "Compassion Focused Group Psychotherapy for people who could attract a diagnosis of personality disorder"
By Kate Lucre

Mood Disorders

Chapter 18: "Compassion Focused Therapy (CFT) for emotion regulation difficulties"
By Chris Irons
Chapter 19: "Compassion Focused Therapy for the treatment of anxiety"
By Dennis Tirch
Chapter 20: "True Strength: Using Compassion Focused Therapy in the treatment of problematic anger"
By Russell L. Kolts
Chapter 23: "Compassion Focused Therapy as an evolutionary and biopsychosocial understanding of depression and its management"
By Gregoris Simos

Eating Disorders

Chapter 22. "The Roles of shame, self-criticism and compassion focused therapy in eating disorders and disordered eating"
By Ken Goss and Allison Kelly

Schizophrenia Spectrum Disorders

Chapter 24: "Compassion Focused Therapy for voice-hearing and delusions in psychosis"
By Charles Heriot-Maitland

Schizophrenia and related disorders are the most prevalent of SMI conditions. The following book and chapter recommendations will help clinicians further understand how CFT can assist in the recovery from psychosis.

Braehler, C., Harper, J., & Gilbert, P. (2013b). "Compassion focused group therapy for recovery after psychosis." In C. Steel (ed.), *CBT for schizophrenia: Evidence-based interventions and future directions* (pp. 235–266). Wiley Blackwell

Heriot-Maitland, C., & Longden, E. (2022). *Relating to Voices Using Compassion Focused Therapy: A Self-help Companion.* Routledge. https://doi.org/10.1080/17522439.2023.2172602

Trauma and Related Disorders

Chapter 25: "Using Compassion Focused Therapy to work with complex PTSD"
By Deborah Lee

Last, it is imperative that therapists understand and attend to ways in which diversity and cultural factors uniquely impact group members. Recent shifts in psychology have led to adoption of multiculturally considerate frameworks, due to the understanding that additional stress and therefore mental burden is experienced by minority individuals. This is especially relevant when working with SMI populations, as literature shows the increased vulnerability to and prevenance of SMI for those with marginalized identities. Recent research indicates that psychotherapy outcomes improve when therapists have higher levels of cultural competence and the ability to adapt therapy and address concerns brought up by clients from diverse backgrounds. It is beyond the scope of this manual to adequately address multicultural proficiency. First, it is recommended clinicians start by becoming familiar with the guidelines on multicultural context, identity, and intersectionality (http://www.apa.org/about/policy/multicultural-guidelines.pdf). Next, it is highly recommended therapists have a thorough understanding of the relationship between multiculturalism and SMI. The following recourse is recommended as a starting point:

Mamani, A. W. d., Gurak, K., & Suro, G. (2014). "Serious mental illness." In F.T.L. Leong, L. Comas-Díaz, G.C. Nagayama Hall, V.C. McLoyd, & J.E. Trimble (eds.), *APA handbook of multicultural psychology*, Vol. 2. Applications and training (pp. 345–359). American Psychological Association. https://doi.org/10.1037/14187-020

Module 1

Introduction, Compassion, and Tricky Brain

REMEMBER: Do not sacrifice the moment for the manual. Be sure to assess and attend to diversity in terms of demographic as well as diagnoses within the group. Be aware of reasons for referral; this will inform fears, blocks, and resistances toward treatment that may arise throughout the duration of the group. This initial awareness of patient presentation and circumstance will allow the group leader(s) to better facilitate cohesion and participation.

Aims:

- Introduce compassion focused therapy (CFT).
- Establish group rules, norms, and safety. Discuss terms and limits of confidentiality within the inpatient setting.
- Define compassion
- Discuss psychoeducation on the tricky brain, genes, and evolution.
- Help participants understand the idea "it's not your fault" while also learning to "take responsibility."
- Help participants understand the concept wisdom about how our minds work as an aspect of compassion.

Welcome Group Members and Set Group Rules

Materials: Handout 1.1

General Principle: There are many exercises in this session. You will not be able to complete all of them, and some can be shortened if needed. When conducting exercises ensure the group has time to process the practice. This may look different depending upon the level of symptoms in the group (e.g., negative and positive symptoms, emotion dysregulation, low cognitive functioning, etc.). If you find yourself speaking for long periods of time when there are low levels of symptomatology, you are probably doing too much. High levels of disengagement due to negative and positive symptoms

DOI: 10.4324/9781003607557-1

may require a more directive approach (e.g., calling on group members for input to either activate them or redirect from internal stimuli). Additionally, repeating important concepts will likely be necessary.

Welcome

Welcome participants to the group and introduce yourself.

Group Overview

> *Welcome to your first compassion focused therapy group. The purpose of our CFT group is to come together and work together to find ways to deal with life difficulties and to learn how to manage distress. In this group we will learn about the impacts that biology, psychology, and social environments have on each of us. Our main goal will be to learn about compassion and how it can improve our lives.*

Set Group Rules

> *Starting a group can seem uncomfortable and even scary. Some of you might not know much about this group or how it might help you, so it's wonderful to see all of you here facing up to this anxiety and uncertainty. Just by being here, you've already shown compassionate courage because you are willing to try out a new treatment.*
>
> *We are all on the same journey of dealing with things that are, and have been, painful. There are things that we may be ashamed about and things that we worry about. In order for this group to be successful, we want it to be a safe place.*
>
> *Before we start doing group work, let's work together to come up with rules that will help all of us feel safe and comfortable in the group. This group will go best if everyone participates, even if it is a little bit scary or hard to do so. Let's think of some rules that might make it easier for everyone to share and feel supported.*

You will likely have to provide some examples of group rules as members might not feel comfortable or know what to say yet. Ask for feedback from the group as you share these rules.

> *Some examples of group rules are "Don't talk over one another," "Listen and support each other," "Be respectful to everyone in the group," etc.*
>
> *What other group rules would help you to feel safe and supported here?* (List on whiteboard.)

Write out the rules the group members come up with. Refer to **Handout 1.1** to have group members discuss additional group rules they may have missed. Have group members write down any rules created that were not included in the list, to refer back to.

The therapist should also make note of group rules that are listed—these should be referred to later.

Next, present potential difficulties for group members to consider; for example, ask the group:

What should the group do if someone becomes upset and wants to leave?

What if someone in the group needs to use the restroom?

What should we do if someone distracted during group?

What should we do if somebody finds it difficult to talk and participate in the group?

What might be do if someone in the group talks a lot and becomes rather dominating?

Confidentiality

Clarify limits of confidentiality. In addition to the typical limits of confidentiality (i.e., imminent danger to self/others or disclosure of abuse), speak to limits in your treatment setting (e.g., group notes will be written that other providers will have access to, disclosure of breaking setting rules may be addressed, etc.).

Introductions

Now that we have established some ground rules to help us feel safe with each other, we can introduce ourselves to each other and say a bit about our hopes and fears of coming to the group. Let's start by thinking about:

What do you hope to gain from coming to a compassion focused therapy group?

Some group members might be there simply because they were signed up and told to attend; some may not know what they want to get out of group aside from meeting facility expectations. Acknowledge this and welcome these participants regardless.

Is there something you might be worried about?

"Me Too" Exercise

As members share what they hope to get out of the group or what they are worried about, ask others to raise their hands if they share that same hope/fear. This might also be done by having group members stand in a circle and step to the center when also feeling or thinking something that was shared. It is often helpful when group leaders also participate during the exercise. This bridges to the important element of common humanity, a way for group members to begin feeling they are not alone. This exercise will give all group members, even those who might be hesitant, an opportunity to participant.

Help participants understand that in CFT, we are asking participants to share their story with us. This will help build narratives, help the group connect, and create opportunities for a sense of common humanity. By sharing we begin to realize that we are all more like than we are different.

CFT Overview

Materials: Handout 1.2

Let me explain a little bit about how this group works. In our group we will learn about the body and the mind and how they interact with others (i.e., a bio-psycho-social model). In each session we'll be spending a little time learning some important CFT skills. We expect that you will practice the skills and exercises we cover in group outside of group. Our goal in this group is to increase wisdom and understanding of how our brain and past experiences affect us. In each group we want to help you to apply the content and skills to your own personal life outside of group. In short, we want to hear from you about how CFT is working, or not working, for you so that our group is personally relevant.

Today we're going to learn what compassion is and is not and introduce three core qualities of compassion—strength, wisdom, and commitment. We will continue to talk about these three qualities through our group. We are also going to spend time understanding more about the human brain which turns out to be very tricky.

CFT Definition of Compassion: What Compassion Is and Is Not

Take a moment to think about the word compassion. What examples of compassion have you seen? Do you know any compassionate people? How do they act and what kinds of things do they say?

Write the answers group members give on the whiteboard and process with the group; recognize themes or qualities related to compassion that members bring up. Allow sufficient time to allow group members to explore their own current understanding of compassion and experience with compassion. This may be difficult for some group members who have received little compassion in life.

Validate the intuitive wisdom of the group for the answers they provide. Do not erase the answers, as you will be using them later. Using the whiteboard, you might make lists of what compassion is and is not.

At the same time, you can have group members turn to **Handout 1.2** to follow along on what compassion is and is not as you go through the following content.

Compassion Is Not

Compassion is not just being nice . . .

If your group members described compassion as being kind, nice, etc., validate that this answer is understandable because compassion is often delivered in a kind manner. Then provide the following education.

Compassion is more than being nice. For example, it your friend is scared to go out and be around others, what is the compassionate thing to do? Is it to say "okay" and allow your friend to stay in day after day? Or is it to help your friend try each day as best they can to go out, even though it might be difficult? Why is the second more compassionate? Compassion also includes wisdom and courage, which means we have to have the wisdom that the hard and difficult route might be the compassionate route and the courage to take that route.

Process.

Compassion is not just feeling sorry for people. Compassion is not just a feeling but an action. You may feel sorry for people, but compassion comes when there is a commitment to help others. Remember, one of the qualities of compassion is commitment.

Process.

Compassion is not being submissive. In fact, compassion can be assertive. Does that feel right? Compassion is not just giving in and submitting. Sometimes being compassionate means standing up for yourself or others.

Process.

Compassion is not just about love. It's easy to be compassionate with those we do love, but compassion for those we don't love or like can be hard. Compassion doesn't mean we have to like everyone. Again, we might not like the person or want to turn them into a friend, or even see them again, but we can still be compassionate.

Process.

Compassion is not weak. As a matter of fact, compassion takes strength. Sometimes saying no to someone we love when it is in their or our best interest can be hard and take courage, but it is the compassionate thing to do.

Process.

Why might we not want to be compassionate? Are there reasons we might reject compassion from others as well?

Begin to identify potential roadblocks group members experience related to experiencing compassion. Some responses may be rooted in misperceptions of compassion (e.g., "Being compassionate is hard because it makes me look weak," "Being compassionate toward yourself or others is hard when you rarely receive compassion," etc.).

Summarize the Definition of Compassion

Let's put all these ideas into a single sentence and define compassion:

Compassion is sensitivity to suffering and distress in self and others, with a commitment to try to alleviate and prevent it.

One insightful group member in another group summarized this by saying, "Compassion is empathy in action," meaning compassion is both feeling and acting. (Write these definitions on the write board and encourage group members to write this in Handout 1.2.)

There are two parts to the definition; first, feeling and, second, taking action.

You may further highlight the two aspects of compassion by using examples. For example, if you met with your doctor and shared how you have been feeling sick, you would need both treatment and comfort. If you doctor gave you only one or the other, you would not feel better.

Provide your own example.

Process.

What Compassion Is

There are three key qualities that help enable the development of compassion: (1) wisdom, (2) strength, and (3) commitment. (Write these qualities on the whiteboard.)

Wisdom means knowing how things are, knowing you have a tricky brain, and that you were raised in an environment that you didn't choose; it allows you to cut yourself some slack and have compassion for yourself.

Strength means having the courage to take responsibility and work with your distress.

Commitment means you are going to follow through with things, long term. Commitment means you will aim to apply CFT in your life.

You will be returning to the ideas of wisdom, strength, and commitment over and over throughout the group, so be sure to embed these in the minds of the participants.

Have group members write down any additional defining features of what compassion *is* or *is not* to **Handout 1.2.**

Compassion to Others (Optional)

This optional exercise (provided at the end of the module) helps group members to better explore their understanding of compassion by thinking about a time when they helped another person.

Compassion from Others (Optional)

This optional exercise (provided at the end of the module) helps patients explore how it feels to receive compassion from others.

Psychoeducation on the Tricky Brain, Genes, Evolution

Materials: Handout 1.3
Handout 1.4

> **Note for the Group Leader**
>
> These handouts provide summaries or imagery of psychoeducation you will cover in this section. Encouraging participants to have this open will be helpful, but you do not need to cover everything directly from the handouts. Other handouts in the following modules are similar; they are intended to provide each group member with organized visual information. These handouts can help patients follow along in the moment and allow patients to refer back in the future.

Compassionate Wisdom

Let's return to compassionate wisdom and explore it in more detail. Wisdom is based on understanding and knowledge. The more we know about our minds and why they are the way they are, the more we can engage with suffering and work out what to do. Let's look more into wisdom.

The human body and mind have all kinds of difficulties wired into them through no fault of our own. Think about the human body first.

For example, many animals walk on all fours because that's how skeletons are built. Humans evolved to walk upright on two legs. That has the advantage of leaving our hands free and enabling us to see more. This has some big disadvantages too. Many humans have back and knee problems because we walk up right.

Like the human body, the human brain is imperfect as well. While our human brains have evolved to do amazing things animal brains cannot do, our human brains can also cause us trouble. Our minds (like our bodies) have evolved to be different from animals. We have a "new brain," which is trickier. We have developed the capacity to do more than just feel—we can also think and use our brains in complex ways. But because our brain is trickier, we need to learn how to manage it.

Process.

Try to be thoughtful and create your own examples to highlight what you are teaching. Group members will likely be more engaged and better understand concepts when the examples provided are relatable and relevant to them. Many patients have probably never thought about the fact that the human brain is not well designed. You're introducing this idea early to support the idea that things are "not your fault." Patients may benefit from a visual representation of the brain—including the "new brain" (thinking) and the "old brain" (emotions/feeling).

Before we discuss more about the brain and how it works, let's talk about an example. Think about learning to drive a car.

Here, the leader can check in to see how many patients have driven a car. In inpatient settings, it is possible that not many have learned to do so. In that case, using a similar example specific to the setting you are in (e.g., to get discharged from the hospital, you have to know a bit of how it works).

What do you need to know in order to drive a car?

Process. Many answers will be provided.

We need to know what the brakes do and how to use them, what the gears are and how to move through them, what the steering wheel does and how to work it, etc. We even get driving lessons from somebody to practice and bring it all together.

It is the same with the human brain—we need to know a bit about how it works so we can understand it and "use" it effectively. Has anyone told you about how our brains got to be the way they are and how they work? Have you thought about what human brains are set up to do? Did anybody ever tell you that our brains don't always work that well? Sometimes we may forget that our brains can be very tricky things and start to blame ourselves for what our tricky brains naturally do.

We Are Socially Constructed by Our Experiences

Like many other animals, we have powerful emotions and desires partly because our genes built them into us. This is part of being human. But our genes do not predict every part of our life.

For example, imagine you were born into a different family or born in a different country. Your brain would be built different from how it is today because of this different background. You would be a different "version" of yourself than you are today because of a different background.

But consider this: To what extent did I have control of my circumstances and how life played out? This is the tricky thing. To some extent, all of us have been created in a unique way and each of us have had experiences we could not control. Part of what we're trying to do with compassion focused therapy is to learn this wisdom and start choosing the version of ourselves we want to become. In compassion focused therapy, we work toward developing the compassionate version of ourselves.

Wisdom is important because if we begin to understand ourselves better, we can begin to choose to be a better version of ourselves. We can begin to develop a mind that is able to deal with the pain and suffering we all carry.

You may ask patients to refer to **Handouts 1.3** to review the points discussed.

Process.

Loops in the Mind and the Relationship Between Mind and Body

What can you do that most other animals can't?

Process and write the responses on the whiteboard.

Here are some of the things you could write if not covered by the group:

We can think and reason.
We can ruminate, or run things over and over in our mind.
We can be creative.
We can anticipate the future.
We have a sense of self.
We can try and think about what other people are thinking about us.
We can empathize with other people.

There are so many things that our brain allows us to do that animals can't do. Many of these things are what make our brain incredible! But without caution, we can have all kinds of problems with it. Let's talk about this.

Process.

Guide group members to thinking about differences, such as self-awareness and how different that is from animals. This sense of self leads us to do things that animals don't—we judge ourselves, like or dislike ourselves, and criticize ourselves.

Old Brain vs. New Brain

Zebra Example: It is recommended the therapist use their own personal example to illustrate this principle, this is typically more engaging for group members. Using a domestic or local animal that members are likely all familiar with would be ideal (e.g., a dog, cat, deer, etc.). When creating your own example, it is important to emphasize how the "old brain," or animal brain, is no longer concerned with a stressful event after safety is reached. Humans, on the other hand, with their "new brain," will continue to think about, tell stories about, and experience emotions tied to the event.

Let's consider a specific example. Imagine a zebra running away from a lion. In the moment the zebra would feel very alarmed. Once the zebra gets away and can no longer see, hear, or smell the lion, there is nothing to keep it anxious. In fact, it would calm down quite quickly. While a human would also be relieved to escape a lion, their new brain will continue to ruminate and spin. A human might think, "Can you imagine if I had been caught? What would it be like to be eaten by a lion? What if there are two lions tomorrow? What if my family were to also get eaten by the lion? What if . . . what if . . . what if . . . what

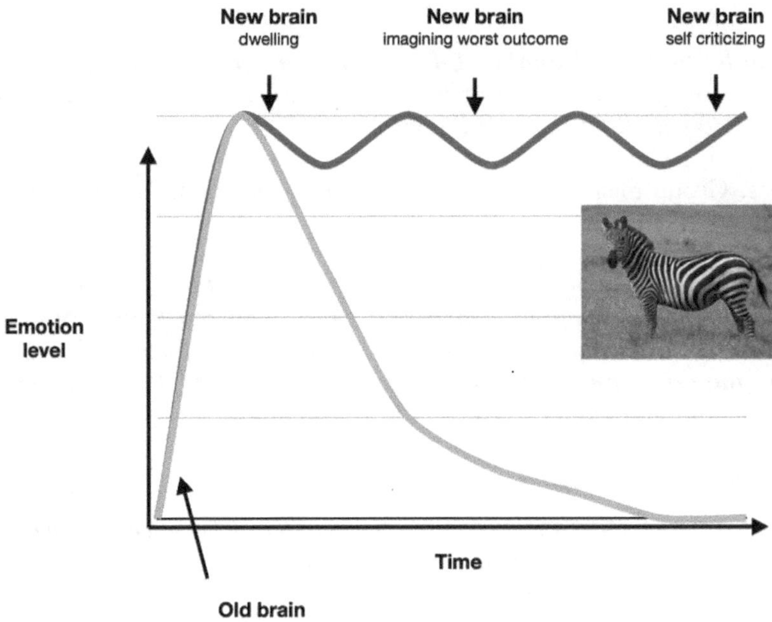

Figure 1.1 Old brain vs. new brain

if . . . ?" The new brain will keep us feeling anxious and on guard. Zebras do not do anything like this!

As humans, we have a different type of mind. We share many desires with animals (to eat, have relationship, be safe, have offspring, etc.), but we have this new mind, which enables us to be self-aware and to self-monitor. With this new brain, we can think a lot about the past and future. Our brains can be complicated, and we often forget that it's not our fault that our brains are this way. We did not choose to have this type of brain. However, it is our responsibility to learn about our minds and learn how to use them. Although our new brains can be tricky, they are also capable of amazing things.

In compassion focused therapy we will also focus on the fact that our new brains go in loops and that these loops can be changed if they are unhelpful.

All of this leads us to the conclusion that we don't have to be stuck with the version of ourselves that we are. Change is possible. We can begin to think about the version of the self we want to become and work toward that.

Process.

Mind-Body Connection

> ***Now let's look at Handout 1.4. Imagine for a moment a ripe yellow lemon. Imagine taking a big bite out of this lemon and chewing it up. What do you notice in your body?***

Process. Group members may say things like salivation, muscle tension, pursed lips, squinting eyes, etc.

> ***This simple example highlights how the mind and body are interconnected. By just imagining something your body can have a physical reaction. One thing we will focus on in compassion focused therapy is how our minds and bodies are interconnected. We will be able to better understand our emotions by noticing our bodies.***

Compassionate Wisdom

> ***One of the first steps in becoming the version of ourselves we want is to acknowledge our compassionate wisdom. This is the wisdom that we are all built by genes and shaped by life events that we do not have control over. It's not our fault that we were built the way we are. All the suffering and difficulties we have had to face—these are not your fault.*** (30 seconds of silence.)

Let group members sit with that in silence for at least 30 seconds. This can be extremely moving for some people while others may be avoidant. If people come up with objections, acknowledge them, and, as best you can, help them focus on the basic principle. Remind them that this is not about avoiding responsibility but embracing it.

> **Note for the Group Leader**
>
> It is important to clearly summarize, and at times repeat, main points of the session as many group members may find it difficult to process and remember information. Some patients may attempt to connect or conflict the CFT content covered with other therapeutic modalities. It is important to integrate treatment and find ways for patients to merge this new information with existing "wisdom" from other group treatments.

Examples for Introducing "Responsibility" (Optional)

Two optional examples are provided at the end of the module to help patients better understand the concept of responsibility. The first example is about fixing your car when it has been damaged by another person. The second example is about positive symptoms (i.e., hearing voices).

Reviewing Compassion Process

Jordan is a made-up patient meant to help group members apply what they have learned during the session to a realistic situation. Applications from previous sessions may be reviewed before the paragraph corresponding to the current module if deemed appropriate. However, often going straight to the paragraph for the module is sufficient, particularly when time is short. Group leaders may present Jordan as female by altering pronouns if seen as appropriate or beneficial for the group. The narrative may be altered to better reflect the structure of your particular treatment setting. For the full Jordan story, see Appendix B.

> *We will be talking about a made-up person named Jordan. One day, Jordan was sitting out in the dayroom when a fight broke out between a new patient and another patient. With all the commotion, it was unclear who started the fight and who was involved once staff showed up. The new patient blamed Jordan, as well as everyone else in the dayroom. The nurse decided everyone present would receive consequences and decided to drop everyone's level.*
>
> *Let's apply what we have learned today to Jordan. Jordan has a tricky brain just like everyone else. He was born with a brain and genes that he didn't choose. He was also born into circumstances he didn't choose. These circumstances have influenced who he has become. When Jordan's level was dropped, he became very angry and disappointed. These emotions are unpleasant, and although Jordan didn't choose to feel them, he does. His mind starts to go in loops, and he repeatedly wonders how things could have been different. Jordan thinks, "I shouldn't have been in the dayroom. I should have stopped the fight from escalating. The staff are so unfair. I'll never get my level up. I've been working so hard and I'm not getting anywhere." These loops make him feel worse, but his brain was built to do this. He did not choose it, and it is not his fault. However, Jordan still tries to take responsibility for his emotions and actions. Jordan reminds himself, "It's not my fault, but it is my responsibility." Jordan also remembers the definition of compassion: Sensitivity to suffering and distress in self and others, with a commitment to try to alleviate and prevent it. He recognizes that having his level dropped is hard for him. Then he starts to use this wisdom that helps him feel better. This is compassion.*

Between-Session Practice

Between-session practices are designed for staff or students to meet with CFT group members between group sessions in order to reinforce principles and practices. These exercises are brief but will allow group members to recall and connect with CFT on the days they don't have group.

How do we define compassion? (Give time for group members to give a definition.) *Compassion is a sensitivity to suffering, with a commitment to alleviate and prevent it. We do exercises to help us with our goal to increase compassion.*

Now let's move into an exercise. As we will talk about in group later, breathing is a tool we can use. As we slow down and focus on our breath, we slow our minds and our bodies down. This helps us move into a state where we are more open to compassion.

We start by closing our eyes or looking down. Notice how it feels to sit on your chair right now. (15 seconds.)

Notice your posture with your back straight and shoulders in line with your hips. Now slow your breath. Try to breathe from your stomach rather than your chest. With each slower and deeper breath, say, with a friendly tone, "Mind slowing down" and then "Body slowing down." Alternate these phrases on each in- and out-breath. Gradually get that sense of grounding with a sense of stilling and slowing but also with alertness in your mind. Notice yourself becoming more grounded.

Allow time for this to settle in. (Longer pause.)

Just connect with the body. Feel your body in the chair at this moment. When you are ready, you can slowly start to come back into the room and open your eyes. (Pause.)

How was that exercise? When might an exercise like this be helpful to you? (Give time to respond.)

Optional Material

CFT Definition of Compassion: Compassion to Others

Since this is a compassion focused therapy group, it's useful for us to think about what we mean when we use the word compassion. In fact, you probably have already had your own insights into what this word means. To help you recognize that you already have some understanding of compassion, think of a time that you tried to help somebody who was having difficulties. Don't focus too much on their distress, but on what was happening in you.

Bring that event to mind. (Pause.)

Group Rules

Respect & Support

- We respect each other and the courage of coming here.
- We try to support each other as best as we can.

Participation

- No pressure to talk if you don't want to.
- If someone is feeling upset, it is okay for us to focus on that before moving on.

Confidentiality

- We agree to keep things only in the group so members can feel safe.
- Remember limits of confidentiality.

Be Open Minded

- We will be open to each others differences.
- We want to make new experiences, so we try to be open to learning.

Between Session Practices

- Practice outside of session is important.
- We will begin each session with a check-in with how your between session practice went.

Other Group Rules

Handout 1.1 Group Rules

Definition of Compassion

Compassion IS...	Compassion is NOT...
...wisdom	...not just being nice
...strength	...not feeling sorry for others
...commitment	...not being submissive
...a sensitivity to suffering and distress with a commitment to alleviate and prevent it	...not just for people we love
...empathy in action	...not weak

Handout 1.2 Definition of Compassion

Handout 1.3 The Tricky Brain

The Mind-Body Connection

What happens in our mind will impact our body.

Imagine biting into a lemon...

Handout 1.4 The Mind-Body Connection

Process.

What were you feeling?

Process.

What were you thinking?

Process.

And what did you want to do?

Process.

CFT Definition of Compassion: Compassion from Others

> **Note for the Group Leader**
>
> You can do this as a large group or in pairs. If there are two group leaders, the leaders can demonstrate the exercise to the group.

To start just get comfortable in your chairs, feet flat on the floor, sitting straight, shoulders back, and chest open; if you are comfortable, gently close your eyes or, if you prefer, just direct your gaze downward.

Everyone has a different life experience and is at a different place with compassion, so let's notice what compassion is like for you.

As we go through this exercise, please go at your own pace and with curiosity. Just notice what unfolds in your mind and body as we go through this exercise.

So just notice how it makes you feel to imagine having somebody like this who really cares about you and supports you. Just sit with that image. Having a felt sense of what it is like to have somebody who is committed to fully understanding, supporting, and encouraging you.

Okay, now you can let that image go. Now I'd like to invite you to see if you can remember a time in your life when somebody was very compassionate to you. The key here is to focus not on any distress you had at the time but on the feelings you had toward somebody who was helpful. What did it look like? (Pause.) *It might be a friend, a family member, a relative, or a stranger. Perhaps even a pet or an animal. It doesn't matter who, but just see if you can find a time when somebody in your life was very compassionate to you. It can be a very small thing that they did or said, or it can be a big thing.*

What do you think was in their mind as they were being compassionate toward you? Why would you define this interaction as compassionate? How did it make you feel?

Okay, now start to let that image and feelings go. Start to come back slowly into the room, noticing our bodies in the chair, feet on the ground, and when you are ready, you can open your eyes.

So how did people find that experience? What did you notice? What feelings inside of you emerged? Did you notice any problems, difficulties, resistances, or worries?

Process.

Psychoeducation on the Tricky Brain, Genes, Evolution: Examples for Introducing Responsibility

Example 1: Parking Lot Example

Suppose while your car is parked in the parking lot, somebody smashes into the back of it and drives off. Then, although this is completely unfair, and you may feel very angry, only you can call the mechanic and get them to come and repair it.

It's your responsibility—it has nothing to do with fairness. We don't like this idea, but unfortunately, it's a fact of life: bad things happen to us that are not fair. We can be very angry about that, understandably, and managing it is still our responsibility.

Process.

Example 2: Positive Symptom Example

Let's say for example you experience hearing voices that other people don't hear. This may be due to genetic and environmental factors that are out of your control, an environment you didn't choose, and a tricky brain. It seems unfair and feels out of your control. At the same time, how do you take responsibility for your life so that these experiences do not cause more pain and suffering?

Process. Reiterate compassionate wisdom, courage, and commitment.

Module 2

Three Systems of Emotion

REMEMBER: Do not sacrifice the moment for the manual. Be sure to assess and attend to diversity in terms of demographic as well as diagnoses within the group. Be aware of reasons for referral; this will inform fears, blocks, and resistances toward treatment that may arise throughout the duration of the group. This initial awareness of patient presentation and circumstance will allow the group leader(s) to better facilitate cohesion and participation.

Aims:

- Introduce soft-landing exercises.
- Review the three systems of emotion: threat (red), drive (blue), and soothing (green).
- Discuss the evolutionary function of these systems.
- Help group members recognize and apply this model to their lives.
- Discuss how compassion relates to the three systems.
- Continue soothing rhythm-breathing practice and compassionate self development.

Welcome, Soft Landing, and Personal Practice

Welcome patients again to the group.

Before the soft-landing exercise begins, explain what it is and why we do it:

> *One of the things we can do to move into a more compassionate self is something called a "soft landing." Soft landings are a kind of guided meditation used in compassion focused therapy. This type of breathing exercise activates the part of the brain that allows us to be calm. Being calm and at peace makes it easier to be compassionate.*

DOI: 10.4324/9781003607557-2

Soft Landing

Today we will do a short soft landing so we can start practicing this skill. To start, get comfortable in your chairs. Put your feet flat on the floor and sit upright with your shoulders back and chest open. If you are comfortable, gently close your eyes. Or, if you prefer, just direct your gaze downward.

Now gently begin to slow down you're breathing. Start to settle your mind and body. Mind slowing down, body slowing down. (Pause.)

Remember the nature of compassion. Compassion means being sensitive to suffering in self and others. It also means being committed to try to lessen and prevent suffering. We are working to develop this more fully in our lives.

With this in mind, try to connect with your compassionate self. Focus on why you are coming here today and over the next several weeks by repeating to yourself the following:

Say in your head, I am coming here today in order to:

- *Develop compassion for myself.* (Pause.)
- *Increase compassion for others.* (Pause.)
- *Be open to compassion from others.* (Pause.)

Now allow yourself to let go of these thoughts. Bring your attention to the sounds in the room. Notice how it feels to be sitting in your chair. And when you feel ready, open your eyes.

What was that like for you?

Process.

Bridge and Forecast

In our last session(s) we focused on our tricky brains and how our brains are not our fault—however, we are still responsible.

> **Note for the Group Leader**
>
> Be mindful of group members with lower cognitive function, active positive or negative psychotic symptoms, or any other symptoms that might interfere with learning. This makes repetition key. The review of the previous session may need to be more detailed by including past examples and a review of psychoeducation. You may need to repeat some of the experiential exercises briefly or review the rationale behind them.

Today we are going to look at three emotion systems that, like our tricky brains, are built in to us. These systems are there for three main reasons: (1) to keep us safe, (2) to help improve, and (3) to let us feel connected to other people and the world around us. We'll be discussing why emotions are important, even if they are unpleasant and even if we don't want them. We will also explore ways to balance rather than ignore or avoid our emotion systems.

Three Systems of Emotion

Materials: Handout 2.1

Discuss the difficulty of emotions and how they guide our actions. Sometimes our emotions feel helpful and accurate; other times this guidance may be getting in the way.

When have you felt that emotions were helpful?

Process.

When have your emotions gotten in the way?

Process.

As you can see, our emotions can be both helpful and harmful. Even though our emotions sometimes get in the way we still need them. In this group, we do not want to get rid of emotions—we just want to deal with them compassionately.

Draw the three-system model on the whiteboard and refer to **Handout 2.1** so patients can follow along. If possible, be sure to use red for threat, blue for drive, and green for soothing.

We have three main emotion systems. They are the threat system (this system keeps us safe), the drive system (this system helps us improve), and the soothing system (this system helps us rest and feel at peace).

What emotions might fit in each of these systems?

Some emotions may fit in multiple circles (e.g., anxiety may be a threat and drive emotion for many).

Again, our emotions have evolved to help us in different ways.

Threat (Red) Circle

Materials: Handout 2.2
Handout 2.3

> *Let's learn more about our red circle or threat emotions (i.e., anxiety, fear, anger, disgust, etc.). These are emotions that try to keep us alive. They are focused on things that are dangerous or "threats." Are any of these emotions pleasant? Why are they critical for our survival?*

Process.

> *When there are threats around, we need to know they are there. Our red emotions help tell our bodies and prepare us to do things that will keep us safe. This system helps us avoid danger, and the system is automatic—for example, if you are threatened, your heart rate will go up, even if you'd rather it didn't. For example, if you see a rattlesnake, you don't stop to think about what to do next, that could get you killed. This system works very quickly because quick action leads to safety. Much like the tricky brain, this can have its advantages and disadvantages.*

Walk patients through and fill out **Handouts 2.2 and 2.3** for themselves. Discuss what participants wrote about the emotions. It may be helpful for the leader to model by personally walking through the handouts with a situation of their own that relates to the corresponding emotions. Point out that our emotions impact our body/feelings, attention/thinking, and behavior. By better understanding our experience in each of these areas we will better understand our experience of the emotions.

Function of Anxiety

(Depending on the needs of your group, you may want to pause between each question and allow space for the group to process.)

> *Let us see how anxiety plays out in us: open to* Anxiety Handout 2.2
> *Now imagine smoke starts coming from under the door right now.*
> *What would happen in your body?*
> *Where would your attention go; what would your mind focus on?*
> *What kind of thoughts would immediately come into in your mind?*
> *What would your behavior be?*

Process.

> *Notice that the threat system is connected to your body, your thoughts, and your actions.*

Function of Anger

(Depending on the needs of your group, you may want to pause between each question and allow space for the group to process.)

> *Let us see how anger plays out in us: open to* Anger Handout 2.3
> *Imaging your favorite pair of shoes does missing. You later in the day find out your roommate took them and have been wearing them all day.*
> *What would happen in your body?*
> *Where would your attention go; what would your mind focus on? What kinds of thoughts would immediately come into your mind?*
> *What would your behavior be?*

Process.

> *Notice again that the threat system is connected to your body, your thoughts, and your actions.*

Note for the Group Leader and Check-In

For many people with severe mental illness emotions are not so straightforward. Whether due to trauma, substance use, psychosis, etc., some group members might be more disconnected from their emotional experience than others. Further, some group members might have complicated or atypical emotional reactions. Although the examples are typically situations that evoke the proposed coinciding emotions, that might not be case for everyone (e.g., a patient might feel mostly sadness if their roommate took their shoes rather than anger). Checking in with group members emotional reactions to each scenario will be important. Make sure to communicate that there is no "right" or "wrong" emotional reactions. Validating different emotional reaction will help to reinforce the idea of the "tricky brain" and still fits with the idea that our emotions serve a function.

Explain Negativity Bias in our Thinking

> *Our tricky brains tend to focus on and remember threats more quickly than we do positive things. Further, we dwell on and hold on to threats more than positives. This is one part of our tricky brain but is a way we stay safe and avoid harm.*

Process.

> *Here is an example of negativity bias . . .*

Example for Anxiety: Noise During the Night

(The example will likely resonate better if the group leader personalizes it.)

> *Imagine you wake up in the night because you hear a sound outside your bedroom window. Logically, you know that it's probably a bird or the wind making the noise, but another part of you might worry somebody is trying to break in. Nonetheless, because of negativity bias, you're likely to jump to the conclusion that the noise could be a threat. You brain is considering that you may be unsafe and thus you focus on negative outcomes.*

Example for Anxiety: Pass in the Hallway

(The example will likely resonate better if the group leader personalizes it.)

> *Imagine you are walking down a hallway and somebody you know seems to avoid you. You jump to the conclusion that they must not like you. This is bothersome because you want to be liked. Your mind focused on this experience as you imagine all of the reasons they may not like you. Later you find out that this person had recently received bad news and was unhappy, which is why they ignored you. All along it had nothing to do with you, yet your tricky brain focused on the possible negative explanations.*

Process.

> *Anger is another emotion that we find it very easy to jump into and then hold on to.*

Example for Anger: Undercooked Chicken

(The example will likely resonate better if the group leader personalizes it.)

> *Say you had a really good day. Throughout the day you had lots of positive experiences; everyone around you was friendly and you were able to do some of the activities you most enjoy. At the end of the day, you go to dinner and have to wait in a long line for your food. Your food finally*

comes, and you are served chicken that is undercooked. You complain, but no one brings you a new dish, so you are stuck with your raw chicken. When you are heading back after dinner what will you be thinking about? (You will probably focus on the one negative experience you had.)

Process.

Later, when you are talking with your friend about your day, what do you think you'll tell them about? (Again, you will probably focus on the one negative experience you had.)

Process.

You likely won't tell them about how most of your day was great; you will probably tell them about the one bad part of the day: dinner. It is normal for our brains to do this. Our tricky brains so often focus on what does wrong rather than what goes right.

Shutting Down (Optional)

This optional discussion about inhibition is provided at the end of the module. This psychoeducation highlights how our threat emotions may lead our minds to freeze or shut down.

Drive (Blue) Circle

Next, our blue circle focuses on drive. The blue system included emotions related to improving, competitiveness, and pursuing goals. This system relates to thriving or accomplishing, rather than avoiding danger.

Function of Excitement (Optional)

Materials: Handout 2.4

(Try to prioritize the threat and soothing handouts. If you run out of time to complete this handout, it may be assigned for homework.)

This handout allows group members to explore their experience of drive.

Soothing (Green) Circle

Materials: Handout 2.5

The green circle, or soothing system, is also connected to positive emotions. The green circle includes emotions related to peace, connection to others, and connection to the world. When animals are not under threat or trying to do things (hunt, eat, build shelters, etc.), they can go into a state of restfulness or calming (remember the zebra example). This is an important capacity because as our body slows down, the mind and body can reorganize and recover.

Function of Peace (Handout 2.5)

(If you run out of time to complete all handouts, some may be assigned for homework.)

Let's try to imagine that you aren't striving for anything or wanting anything, and you are at peace.

What happens in your body?

Where does your attention go? What does your mind focus on? What kind of thoughts come into and then go around in your mind?

What would your behavior be?

Process.

Again, this emotion system has specific effects on your body, thoughts, and actions.

> **Note for the Group Leader**
>
> Some group members might have little experience with soothing emotions, given an overactive threat system. Pay attention to those who struggle with this. Explain how soothing becomes difficult or rare when we spend too much time in the red circle. Again, this is not anyone's fault but by taking responsibility there are things we can do about this imbalance.

The soothing system can help balance the threat and drive systems. It can help us learn to take our foot off the accelerator and slow down. Soothing emotions help us to feel safe, explore, and be creative. When we're feeling threat emotions all the time, it is likely that we aren't soothing often enough. Part of developing balance will be practicing getting into this soothing system.

It's important to remember that each of these systems have an important role. What we want to do is achieve balance between the systems.

Drawing Your Own Three Circles

Materials: Hanout 2.6

Invite participants to draw their own three circles using **Handout 2.6.**

> *Next, draw out your own three circles in proportion to how much time they spend in each circle. For example, if you spend a lot of time in-threat, draw a large circle. If you spend very little time in soothing, draw a small circle.*

Process.

> *What gets you or keeps you in each system?*
> *How do you shift to a different emotion system?*

Process.

Remind patients that the three circles are not always separate and distinct. At times they may overlap. All three systems are important and necessary. Compassion allows us to balance all three.

Stuart Video

Show the Stuart Video (https://youtu.be/VRqI4lxuXAw) to demonstrate creating balance between the three systems.

This video shows how someone who hears voices might apply and benefit from CFT.

Soothing Rhythm-Breathing: Rationale and Practice

Sympathetic and Parasympathetic Systems

> *When we were discussing how our body reacts to the different emotion systems, you may have noticed that some systems stimulate the body, while others calm it. Our sympathetic nervous system is the activator; it gets us ready. Our parasympathetic system acts as the brakes; it calms us down. Ideally, these two systems should work in balance.*
>
> *For example, these systems are working with each other with every beat of the heart. The sympathetic system speeds up your heart, and the parasympathetic system slows it down, from heartbeat to heartbeat. Without a parasympathetic system, your heart rate would be very fast and never slow down; therefore, we need the parasympathetic system to slow things down. We often spend too much time in our threat*

system, where our sympathetic nervous system is dominant. This type of breathing will help us activate our parasympathetic system.

Soothing Rhythm-Breathing Practice (SRB)

Remember, we are interested in balancing our emotions. For many of us, our soothing system does not work as well as we would like it to. We will be working to train and exercise this system.

> **Note for the Group Leader**
>
> The following is a detailed description of SRB, but you can reduce the length as long as you emphasize the importance of body posture and evenness of the breath. With this population, you will need to emphasize that SRB is a building block. It's the first step in strength/courage. Let the group know that this will be a foundation for intentional compassion. This will lead to other exercises that increase compassion for the self and others.

Remember the soft-landing exercise we tried? This practice is similar, called soothing rhythm-breathing. One way to improve parasympathetic functioning and access our green circle is through soothing rhythm-breathing.

Now we are going to try to breathe in a way that can help us become more grounded and feel stable. We use breathing to activate the soothing system. This type of breathing actually changes our brain chemistry. It can move us out of the threat system to a more soothed, calm state. The idea of this practice is to explore how breathing may affect our mood and bodily states.

Find a comfortable sitting position and notice how it feels to sit in your chair. (Pause.)

Now, we will engage our compassionate body posture.

1. *Sit with a straight back. Keep your head upright and your shoulders in line with your hips. Place your feet flat on the floor.*
2. *Lift your shoulders up and slightly backward.*
3. *Find a comfortable position for your hands that will not be distracting to you.*
4. *Breathe into your belly rather than your chest.*

5. *Bring a friendly facial expression to your body posture.*
6. *Gently fix your gaze on a single spot on the floor, or close your eyes if you feel comfortable.*

If you notice yourself getting distracted from what I'm asking you to pay attention to, that's okay and part of what our brain does. Just compassionately bring yourself back to my voice.

First, notice how you breathe naturally. Pay attention to how breathing makes you feel. Notice how the air comes down into your lungs and then out again. Notice your posture while still focusing on your breathing. (Pause.)

Now let's try to change our natural rhythm slightly. This will help activate your soothing system and create changes in your brain and body. Begin to slow and deepen your natural breath. Your breathing should remain even and unforced. Aim for about five seconds in and five seconds out. For some, counting can be helpful. For others that can get in the way. Find what works best for you.

As you develop your rhythm, notice and focus on the feeling of inner slowing with each out-breath.

On each in-breath, say, in your mind, "Mind slowing down." On each out-breath, say "Body slowing down." Continue alternating these phrases throughout the practice in your head. Maintain an alert mind even as you try to become stiller, slower, and more grounded.

As we practice for a moment, pay attention to the experience of even and unforced breathing. (Pause.)

Now, sense the weight of your body resting on the chair. You may notice that you feel heavier. Feel the stableness in your body that comes from both your compassionate posture and a slower and deeper breath. Imagine sitting like a mountain, strong and stable. Notice these feelings of weight and stability in your body. (Pause.)

This is called grounding.

You may have also noticed a sense of stilling during this practice. This feeling of stillness will grow as we continue slowing, stilling, and grounding ourselves throughout the group.

As we bring this practice of soothing rhythm-breathing to a close, connect with your body again. Feel your body in the chair in this moment. Slowly start to come back into the room, and open your eyes when you are ready.

What was this like for you? What was easy, what was difficult? What did you feel in your body? Where did the mind go? What feelings did you experience?

Process.

Check-In

Some patients may find this exercise difficult, boring, or even agitating. It is important to allow these patients to share their honest experience rather than providing expected answers. Validate the difficulties and how it takes time to develop this skill. Link to the three-circle model.

Reviewing Compassion Process

Optional Review

Reviewing Jordan's situation will likely be helpful to make sure everyone remembers the story.

Module 1: Dayroom fight, level drop, anger/anxiety, thinking loops; trick brain, "not my fault but my responsibility"

Let's think of how to apply what we have learned today to Jordan's situation. When Jordan's level was dropped, he got angry. He is in the red circle, or the threat circle. While he is feeling this way, Jordan remembers that every emotion is important and that anger serves a purpose. He does not want to completely get rid of threat emotions (like anger), because they are telling him something important. However, Jordan can appreciate his emotions without remaining in the red circle. One thing he can do to move out of the red circle is soothing rhythm-breathing. To start this, Jordan brings attention to his breathing. He can gradually slow his breathing and ground himself. This helps him feel calm and allows him to move from threat to soothing, into the green circle.

Between-Session Practice

Today we are going to do a soothing rhythm-breathing exercise. Do you remember what soothing rhythm-breathing is and why we do it?

(Give plenty of time for response.) *It is when we focus on our breathing to activate the soothing circle.*

And which circle is the soothing circle?

(Give plenty of time for response.) ***It is the green circle.***

Can you tell me the other two circles?

(Give plenty of time for response.) ***Red is threat, and blue is drive.***

Now let's move into the exercise

Walk group members through the soothing rhythm-breathing exercise found earlier in this module.

Optional Material

Threat (Red) Circle: Shutting Down

Anger and anxiety might drive us to act in order to feel safe, but sometimes when we are threatened, the body does something else—it shuts down! We can freeze up. In the red circle, this is called inhibition.

This commonly happens with feelings of sadness. When we feel sad, we might feel like withdrawing and not doing anything at all. It's still useful to think of this state of mind as a way to protect ourselves—for example, when you withdraw you avoid experiencing more pain.

Think of times when this might have happened to you. Think of when threat emotions might have led you to shut down or avoid. This can happen when we have been trying hard to change our situation and it is not working out or we feel there is just too much to do.

When we begin to shut down, it is a good sign that we have been spending too much time in the threat circle.

Drive (Blue) Circle: Function of Excitement

Materials: Handout 2.4

Let's imagine you have just won a lot of money, or you got your level increased, or you just got something you've been wanting for a long time. What happens in your body?

Where does your attention go? What does your mind focus on?
What kind of thoughts come into and go around in your mind?
What would your behavior be?

Process.

Like threat emotions, drive emotions influence body, thoughts, and actions.

The 3 Circle Model

Each emotion system is important. Compassion helps us to balance our circles.

THREAT (RED) CIRCLE

The threat system is about protection, staying safe, and fight/flight. The red circle is critical to our survival. However, we often let it run the show without realizing it.

examples: anger, fear, anxiety

DRIVE (BLUE) CIRCLE

The drive system is incentive and resource-focused. It drives us to work toward things we want and desire. Often we use the blue circle to manage our red circle emotions.

examples: motivation, excitement

SOOTHING (GREEN) CIRCLE

The soothing system is about settling, grounding, and safeness. It helps us rest, digest and be open. Spending too much time in the red circle can limit our green circle.

example: peace, calm, contentment

Handout 2.1 The Three-Circle Model

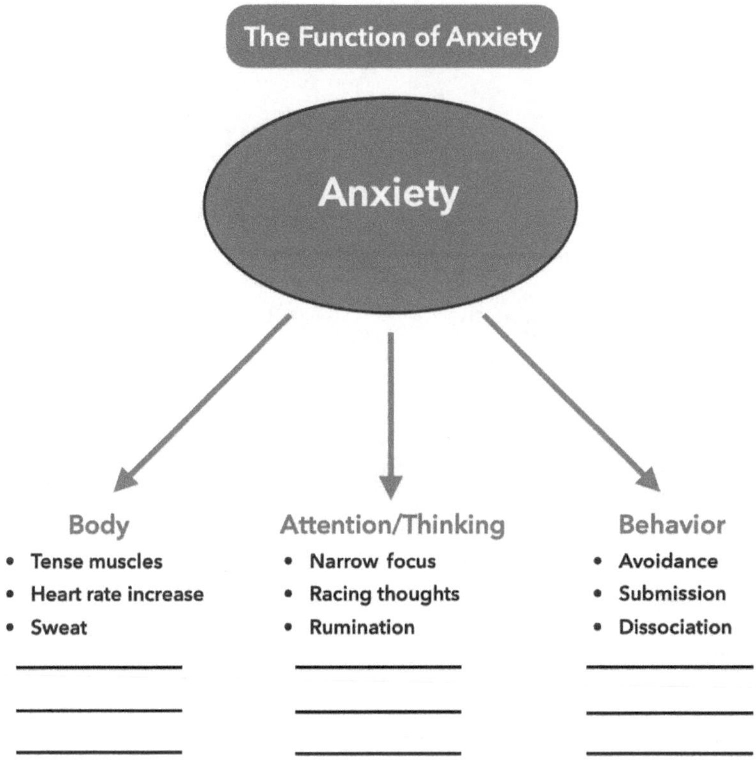

Notes:

Handout 2.2 The Function of Anxiety

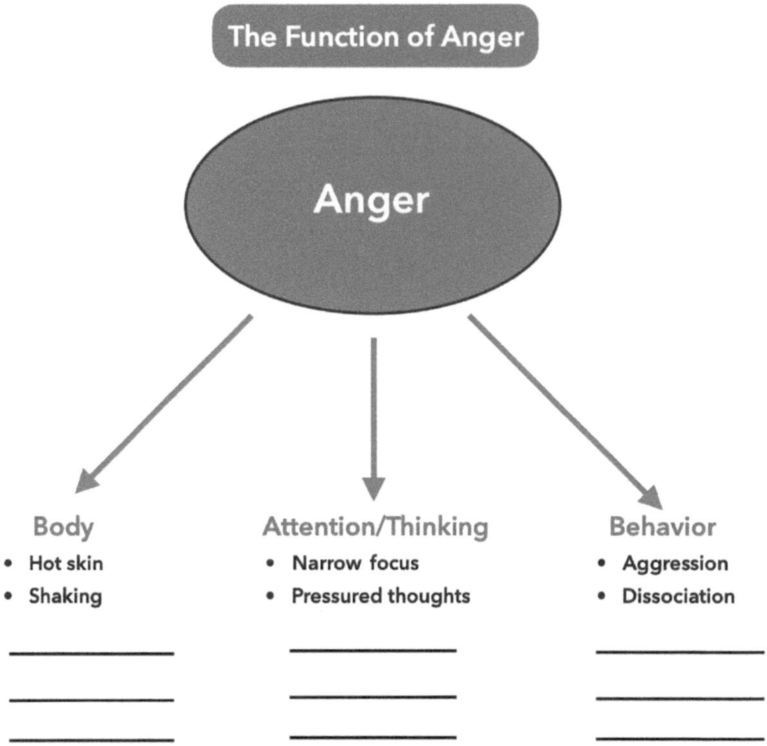

Notes:

Handout 2.3 The Function of Anger

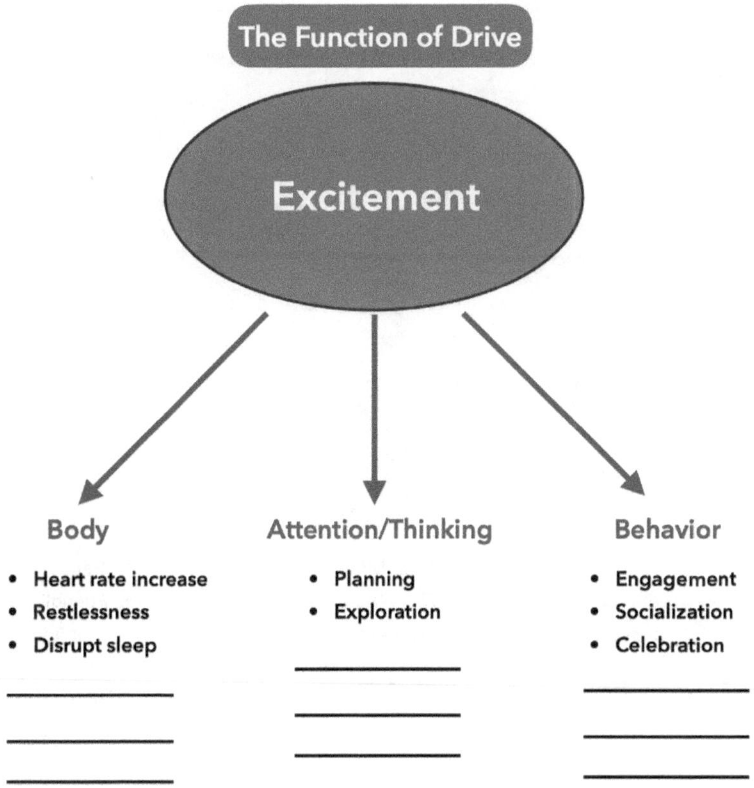

Notes:

Handout 2.4 The Function of Drive

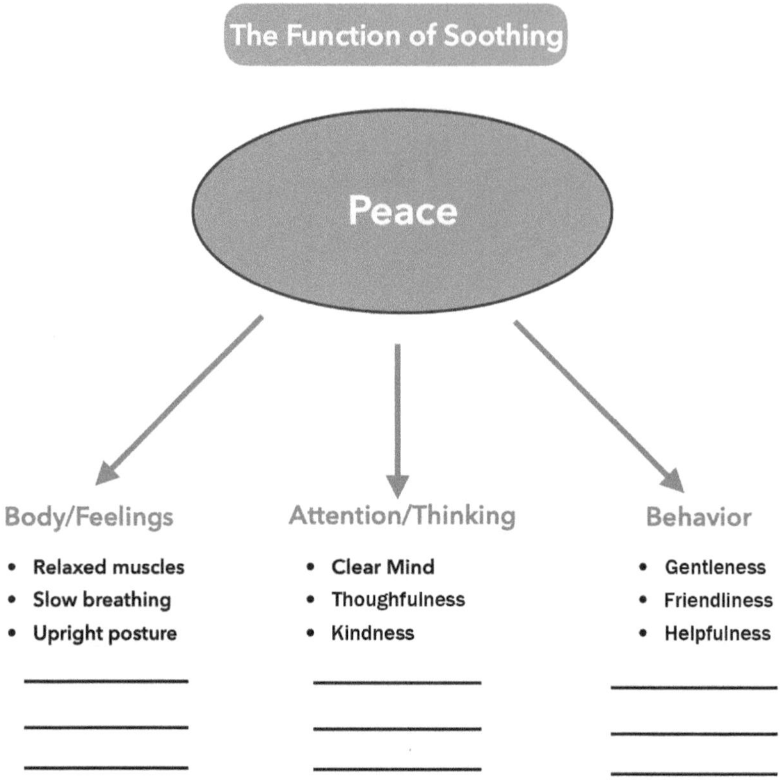

Notes:

Handout 2.5 The Function of Peace

Draw Your Own 3 Circles

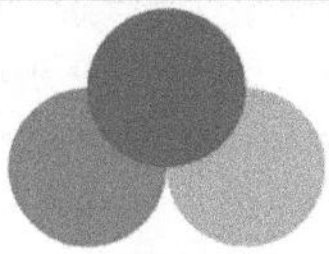

* Which circle do you spend the most time in?
* Which circle do you spend the least time in?
* Are your 3 circles balanced OR imbalanced?

Handout 2.6 Draw Your Own Three Circles

Notice that even thinking about having good things happen to you can activate your body. Our minds are powerful in this way. This is important because as we will note later there are different ways that we can activate the body by intentionally choosing what we focus on.

It is important to remember that sometimes our threat system and our drive system mix together. For example, achievement can be motivated by avoiding something negative rather than building something positive. This can make it hard to learn how to cope with the ups and downs of life. It can also make it hard to have compassion for ourselves and others. Having this wisdom of how our emotion systems mix together will help us as we learn how to have more compassion.

Module 3

Attention Training and Mindfulness

General Principle: There are many exercises in this session. You may not get to all of them, some can be shortened if needed. Be sure to give time for group processing and to emphasize the core principles. This may include asking specific questions or being directive during activities. An example of this behavior during session might look like: "Jim, what emotion did you label? How did you notice it in your body?" Jim responds, "Sadness," to which you might respond, "That is mindfulness. You shined your flashlight on the emotion and noticed it."

There is also lots of psychoeducation in this session. Negative symptoms are often associated with impaired executive and difficulty initiating behavior. Asking individual group members for specific information may allow them to engage with the session material. Try to avoid long periods of explanation.

Aims:

- Introduce attention; help group members understand we can "pay attention" to attention.
- Introduce mindfulness and its cycle and benefits.
- Use various mindful experiences to teach concepts.
- Help group members understand how mindfulness helps us manage emotions.

Welcome, Soft Landing, and Personal Practice

Note for the Group Leader

During soft landings, group leaders often help patients slow their breath and find a steady rhythm through counting. When counting, make sure that you maintain a steady rhythm. When reading the

DOI: 10.4324/9781003607557-3

practice, it is tempting to pause at certain points, like this: "In, 2, 3, pause. Out, 2, 3." This can be confusing for patients and lead to unsteady breathing when pauses are inconsistent. Count as if someone is keeping a beat: "In, 2, 3, 4. Out, 2, 3, 4." This helps the patients follow along and develop a stable rhythm.

Welcome participants to the group.

Soft Landing

We will begin by practicing soothing rhythm-breathing. This is meant to help us become more familiar with how breathing affects the body. You may notice yourself getting distracted. That's normal. When you notice that, just come back to what I'm saying.

Get comfortable in your chairs with your feet flat on the floor, posture upright, and shoulders back so that your chest opens and frees up your stomach. Notice the curve in your back. When you are comfortable, gently close your eyes. Or, if you prefer, just direct your gaze downward.

Breathe more slowly and deeply than you would normally. Try to connect with your mind and body.

Focus on the sensations of breathing, with the air coming in through your nose, down into your stomach, staying a short while, and then moving back out through your nose. Notice how your belly moves gently as you breathe in and out. You might put a hand on your belly to notice.

I will count you into this by saying: "In, 2, 3; out, 2, 3. In, 2, 3, 4; out 2, 3, 4. In, 2, 3, 4, 5; out, 2, 3, 4, 5." (Count about 1 second apart—remember to keep your counting steady.)

When you breathe out, let your breath be a gentle smooth exhale rather than anything forced. Imagine a paper bag releasing air gently and smoothly.

It is important to find your own rhythm. Find a rhythm that helps you slow and settle. As you develop your rhythm, notice and focus on the feeling of inner slowing with each out-breath. Each time you breathe out, say internally in a friendly and supportive voice:

"Body slowing down."

"Mind slowing down."

When you say these words, say them slowly. With each outbreath, each word should take a bit longer to say—until the three words basically use up the five seconds of breathing out of breathing out.

Try to notice how your body responds to your breathing. Find a rhythm within your body that is soothing and calming to you. Feel this not just as breathing but as an inner rhythm.

Let's practice this slower, steadier breathing for 1 minute. You can continue to count for yourself if that is helpful. Or just notice the experience of smooth and even breathing. (1 minute.)

Your mind will probably wander because that's what minds are designed to do. Simply notice it happening and gently guide your attention back to an awareness of your body. Breathe steadily in and out; notice the flow of air coming in and out of your nose. Just gently observe; allow things to be as they are. Feel your body slowing down and your mind slowing down.

Let's remember the nature of compassion. Compassion is sensitivity to suffering in self and others, with a commitment to try to alleviate and prevent it. Keep this in mind as we connect with our compassionate motivation.

I'm going to read you three phrases. As I read them, imagine what each means and what it would be like to live this way. Try to be specific to your situation.

I am coming here today and over the next weeks in order to:

- *Develop compassion for myself.* (Pause.)
- *Increase compassion for others.* (Pause.)
- *Be open to compassion from others.* (Pause.)

Okay, now start to let these thoughts and motivations go. Start to come back slowly into the room. Notice your body in the chair and your feet on the ground. When you are ready, you can open your eyes.

Welcome [back] to Module 3.

Between-Session Practice Check-In

Check that group members were able to engage in between-session practice. Help the group process their experience other the past week, both successes and resistances. You may want to ask those who didn't participate why they didn't perhaps they were anxious about the practices, find the breathing exercises difficult, or think that breathing and mindfulness are silly, etc.

Process.

Bridge and Forecast

Review key ideas from Modules 1 and 2 (tricky brain and three circles) and introduce key ideas of Module 3 (ways we can build our green circle).

> *In Module 1 we learned about our tricky brains and how our brains sometimes make life difficult for us. Last time we built on our understanding of the tricky brain by looking at our three emotion systems: the red, blue, and green circles. We also watched the Stuart Video and practiced soothing rhythm-breathing. Today we will be learning how we can develop our green circle. We're going to learn how to focus our attention, which can be like a flashlight that illuminates what it shines on. Most brains go through a cycle of paying attention and losing focus. Today we'll introduce a model of mindfulness to help you become more aware of your own cycle of attention.*
>
> *We're going to focus on the skill of noticing. This skill can help us to notice which circle we are in and label emotions. Being able to label our emotions increases our ability to balance and cope with them. We'll also practice skills related to facial expression and voice tone, noticing how they stimulate and balance emotions.*

Introduction to Attention

Attention as a Spotlight: Experiential Exercise

> *Please close your eyes or cast your eyes downward. Sit for a moment and pay attention to your left foot. Notice the feelings in your toes and sole of this foot. Be curious.* (5 seconds.) *Now, switch your attention to your right foot.* (5 seconds.) *Now, rub your thumbs over your fingers. Notice the feelings in your hands and fingers as you do this. Remain curious.* (5 seconds.)

You can continue this experience of attention by making it more "real." Turn off or dim the lights in the room and use a flashlight to direct light around the room. Have group members focus on and follow the flight.

> *Next, pay attention to this light. Pay attention to what you notice.*

Turn the lights back on to process.

> *What did you notice during that exercise? Where did your attention go? What did you focus on?*

Process.

> *Our attention can be moved on purpose. While we focus on some things, other things drop out of our attention—like how a spotlight illuminates a specific area.*

Outcomes of Attention

> *We can shift attention not only to our surroundings or current moment, but also to our memories, emotions, and thoughts. When we direct our attention; our body and mind change accordingly. Being stuck in our threat system (red circle) can be very hard for this reason. When we are stuck in threat our attention gets stuck on things that are difficult, painful, or overwhelming. When we practice directing our attention, we can better notice what is going on inside our tricky brain. By doing this, we can also learn how to direct our attention away from threat at times and toward compassion.*

Attention on Negative and Positive Memories (Optional)

This optional exercise, provided at the end of the module, helps group members notice how their body responds when they turn their attention to positive and negative memories.

Introduction to Mindfulness

Materials: Handout 3.1
Handout 3.2

Autopilot

> *Can you remember a time when you were traveling home (walking or riding the bus or driving), and when you arrived, you couldn't quite remember how you got there? This can happen often as your mind can shift into "autopilot."*

Check in to see if group members are familiar with the word "autopilot." If some are not, provide a supplemental definition.

> *There is a reason our minds do this. Being in autopilot can help us save energy doing things we do every day. For example, life is easier when*

you don't have to think much about getting dressed in the morning, eating dinner, or showering. Although going into autopilot can be helpful, at times it can make things difficult. As we just learned, our mind can focus attention on negative or "threat" experiences. This way of directing our attention can become automatic.

Cycle of Mindfulness

The good news is, we can pay attention to our attention; this is mindfulness. Mindfulness we can avoid falling into autopilot. For example, if you feel angry, you don't need to go into autopilot and behave aggressively. With mindfulness, you can recognize your emotion and intentionally apply what we are learning in group (e.g., soothing rhythm-breathing). Mindfulness helps us to be aware of our emotions, thoughts, and actions.

Mindfulness allows us to hold things in our mind, be curious, and explore them from an observer's point of view. Shining your mental flashlight is how we are mindful which allows us to notice the cycles our brain gets into.

Have group members turn to **Handout 3.1** to follow along as you write the diagram on the whiteboard.

The cycle of mindfulness is remembering to pay attention, getting lost to distraction, noticing your distraction, then redirecting your attention. When you are being mindful, you cycle through each of these stages.

Note that getting distracted is a normal part of the cycle of mindfulness. Assure group members that it is okay and expect for distractions to happen—mindfulness just means noticing distractions and redirecting your attention.

Check-In

It is likely that many or most group members have learned about and tried mindfulness in other group or individual treatments. Check in with group members to see if they have been exposed to mindfulness already through other therapeutic modalities. See what they have learned and liked or disliked. Integrate these past or current experiences with your instruction of CFT mindfulness.

Mindfulness Experiential Exercises

Guide participants through the mindfulness exercise of open awareness, then go through some of the optional mindfulness activities best suited for your group. The open awareness exercise is a great introduction to mindfulness and can help clear up concerns or questions.

Open Awareness

> *Sit quietly in your chair and try to find a breathing rhythm that is comfortable and natural to you. Bring your attention to your body.*
>
> *Notice the sensations that are present in your body. You may notice sensations of pressure (such as the weight of your body against the chair), tension (perhaps in your shoulders and neck), or comfort (such as your clothes on your body). Notice any vague sensations, like tingling or twitching. Notice any other sensations, such as sounds or smells in the room.*
>
> *Rest in this awareness of your body, noticing these different sensations. Notice your mind resting in your body and your body resting on the chair.*
>
> *If your mind wanders, that is perfectly fine; that is what minds do. It might wander off to thoughts like "What are we doing?" "Am I doing this right?" or "What am I doing with the rest of my day?" When you notice your thoughts wander like this, just gently notice the distraction and come back to the exercise of attending to your body.*

Process.

Explore difficulties and resistances, and then validate all experiences. This may be an opportunity to link to the three circles. Some members might be so focused on getting mindfulness "right" that the blue circle becomes activated. For others, the red circle may be activated in the form of anger, frustration, or worry about not being able to do it. Explore this.

Other (Optional) Mindfulness Exercises

Use the following optional exercises based on the needs of the group and clinical judgment.

Mindful Eating (Optional)

This optional exercise, provided at the end of the module, is for patients to try mindful eating.

Mindful Walking (Optional)
This optional exercise, provided at the end of the module, is for patients to attend to their surroundings as they walk around the room.
Other Mindfulness Exercises (Optional)
(Depending of the resources of the site)
Other mindfulness exercises can be created and used (e.g., painting, listening to music, spending time in nature, etc.).

All of these exercises can be found in **Handout 3.2** for patients to reference and practice outside of group.

Mindfulness and Emotions (Optional)

The following are more complicated exercises compared to others mentioned. These exercises connect mindfulness to emotional experience. Use if the level of functioning of those in the group permit.

Emotion Labeling (Optional)
This optional section is provided at the end of the module. This exercise has group members label the emotion of anxiety as they reflect on an anxious event. Group members learn that naming an emotion can help them move out of autopilot, and thus be less reactive and controlled by threat emotions.
Emotions Running the Show (Optional)
This optional section is provided at the end of the module. This exercise allows group members and the leader to provide real world examples of threat emotions taking over. Contracting examples are provided of mindfully noticing and labeling emotions, then using aspects of CFT to change course.
Body Posture, Facial Expression, and Voice Tone (Optional)
This optional section is provided at the end of the module. This exercise highlights how our body posture, facial expression, and voice tone are connected to and can perpetuate the emotions we feel.

Reviewing Compassion Process

Reminder

You can review the Jordan content from previous modules as needed, or you can go straight to the example from this module. Often a review is not necessary when time is short, and briefly apply the skills learned that day to Jordan's situation is sufficient.

Optional Review

Module 1: Dayroom fight, level drop, anger/anxiety, thinking loops; trick brain, "not my fault but my responsibility"
Module 2: Jordan's red circle scenario (anger); three circles, soothing rhythm-breathing

Now let's think of how to apply what we have been learning today to Jordan's situation. A few days after the dayroom fight, Jordan still thinks about his level being dropped. His attention is stuck on the past. When his attention is on his level, he stays angry. This is because our attention affects our emotions. Jordan remembers that he can change his emotions by shifting his attention. He notices that when he is focused on his level, he gets angry. As he realizes this, he tries to shift his focus to his breathing. Jordan wants to be in the present moment rather than stuck in the past. As he shifts his attention, he starts to feel calmer and at peace. He uses his attention as a tool to notice and balance his emotions. Using your attention this way is an important part of mindfulness.

Between-Session Practice

Revisit concepts of attention of mindfulness. Review briefly the cycle of mindfulness. Remind participants that getting distracted during the following exercise is normal and part of the process. The goal is to just be aware of this and redirect attention.

Compassionate Body Posture, Voice Tone, and Body Expression

Let's try to apply what we have learned in in group so far. To start, think of a small life difficulty. Make sure you chose something small, like someone saying no to you or losing a belonging. Try not to think about anything too extreme or heavy.

Let's begin by trying to get comfortable. Go ahead and sit upright, and gently close your eyes, or if you prefer, direct your gaze downward.

Now, bring to mind the small life difficulty that you have gone through recently. Let your body take the posture that it naturally takes when you are thinking about that negative event or disappointment. For example, a disappointed posture might have slumped shoulders.

Notice what emotions come up in you as you think about your challenge. (Pause.)

Notice how your body feels. Do you feel tense, anxious, angry, sad, etc.? (Pause.)

Notice what thoughts you have your negative event. (Pause.)

Now we're going to try to switch our attention as best we can. As you think of this negative event, I want you to gently move into a more compassionate body posture.

1. *Sit with a straight back. Keep your head upright and your shoulders in line with your hips. Place your feet flat on the floor.*
2. *Lift your shoulders up and slightly backward.*
3. *Find a comfortable position for your hands that will not be distracting to you.*
4. *Breathe into your belly rather than your chest.*
5. *Bring a friendly facial expression to your body posture.*
6. *Keep your gaze fixed gently on a single spot on the floor or remain with your eyes closed if you feel comfortable.*

Now let's try to activate our soothing system by doing soothing rhythm-breathing. Begin to slow and deepen your natural breath. Each time you breathe out, say internally in a friendly and supportive voice:

"Body slowing down."
"Mind slowing down."

As you find your rhythm, notice and focus on the feeling of inner slowing with each out-breath. (Pause.)

Remember your intention to become more helpful, friendly, and compassionate. Along with this compassionate intention, remember that life is difficult. We all find ourselves here with a tricky brain that has been shaped by our genes and our life experiences. This is not our fault. This wisdom is part of compassion.

As we bring this practice to a close, connect with your body again. Feel your body in the chair in this moment. Slowly start to come back into the room, and open your eyes when you are ready.

Cycle of Mindfulness

Mindfulness is a practice of noticing and gently returning to the moment–NOT trying to rid one's mind of thoughts.

It helps us to become aware of what's going on in our minds and to bring our minds where we want them to be.

Handout 3.1 Cycle of Mindfulness

Mindfulness Exercises

Mindful Breathing

Mindful Breathing helps you to watch your breath and noticing when you get distracted.

HOW TO DO IT:

- First, get comfortable. Place your feet shoulder-width apart, flat on the ground. You might close your eyes or look down at the ground.
- Next, **gently focus your attention on your breath**. Breathe so that the air fills your lungs. Notice your stomach rising and falling as you breathe in and out. Just notice your breath for about 30 seconds.
- REMEMBER, if your mind wanders, that is normal. The idea is to just watch your breath, and begin to notice when your attention drifts off. When you notice that your attention has left your breath, just gently bring it back to your breath, again and again, over and over.
- **The key is that when our thoughts and emotions come up; we don't judge them; we just notice them as mental events ("Oh… there's another thought") and then come back to the breath.**

Handout 3.2 Mindfulness Exercises

Mindful Eating

Mindful eating can help you to feel grounded and focus on what you are doing in the present.

- You can try this when eating any kind of food.
- First, pay attention to the food's texture and color. Take a few seconds to really examine what the food looks like. Next, feel the food; pay attention to how it feels on your fingers. After this, smell the food and think about its smell. Last, take a bite and focus on this feeling. Think about how the food feels in your mouth and how it tastes.

Mindful Walking

Mindful walking can help you to notice your surroundings and be in the present.

- You can do this inside or outside.
- As you walk, try to notice what is around you. Slowly look up, down, and all around you. As you explore, you can pick things up and observe them. Notice how the place you are in looks, smells, sounds, and feels. Try to use as many senses as you can. As always there is no right or wrong way of doing this, just explore your surroundings.

Other Ways to be Mindful

There are many other ways to be mindful. The goal of these exercises is to help you notice what you are doing in the present moment. This is a way you can feel calm and aware.

- Painting or drawing.
- Listening to music.
- Taking a shower.
- Watching the clouds in the sky.

Handout 3.2 (Continued)

Optional Material

Introduction to Mindfulness: Mindfulness Experiential Exercises

Mindful Eating

You can bring in some fruit, candy, or any other food for this exercise. Here the patients will pay attention to many aspects of the food (e.g., appearance, tactile touch, smell, taste, etc.). They will explore the experience of studying the piece of food and slowly eating it. This is called mindful eating because it's paying attention, on purpose, and in the present moment, to the act of eating.

> ***During this exercise we will be practicing mindfulness by focusing our attention on the different senses while eating. First, pay attention to what the (food) looks like.*** (Pause.)
>
> ***Notice its colors, texture, and shape.*** (Pause.)
>
> ***Next, smell the (food) and notice what it smells like.*** (Pause.)
>
> ***Now you may place the (food) in your mouth, but don't eat it just yet. First, explore how it feels in your mouth.*** (Pause.)
>
> ***Once you have explored it your mouth, you may begin slowly chewing the (food) and noticing what it tastes like. As you do this, try to notice if there are any subtle flavors of this (food) that you have never noticed before.*** (Pause.)

Process.

> ***This exercise is called mindful eating because we are purposely focusing our attention on of eating. We focused on the color, texture, smell, and taste of this (food) in a very particular way in order to explore it fully in the present moment. Notice how this was very different from eating on autopilot.***

Mindful Walking

You can invite participants to mindfully walk around the room—noticing objects, picking them up, and exploring items found in the room. The idea is to learn to be immersed in the activity itself; not thinking about the activity.

Process.

For this exercise, we will practice mindfulness by paying special attention to this room. At times, we become so accustomed to an area that we forget to really notice all the things around us.

To start, I stand up from your chairs and begin to walk around the room. Look around, intentionally noticing all the objects in the room. Are there items in the room that you haven't noticed before? As you notice new objects, you might want to pick them up, noticing their color, texture, and weight. Spend some time exploring. (Pause.)

What did you notice during this practice?

Process.

Introduction to Mindfulness: Additional Mindfulness Exercises

The following are suggestions of additional activities that can be used to walk group members through a mindful experience. Feel free to be creative and create your own mindfulness exercise as you know your group best.

- Mindfully listen to music.
- Mindfully engage with any sense, smell, feel/touch, sight, etc.
- Mindfully paint or draw.

Process.

Introduction to Mindfulness: Mindfulness and Emotions

Emotion Labeling

Remember, the goal of mindfulness is to focus on the present moment, but often our minds get wrapped up in thought and drift toward yesterday or tomorrow. Our mind often maintains distress by focusing on stressful events, which can create the unhelpful cycles in our minds that we discussed earlier. Practicing mindfulness helps us to become aware of what is going on in our minds and then to refocus our attention where we want. Our minds will always get lost and distracted, but it can become easier to refocus our attention through training our mindfulness. We will now do an emotional labeling practice that helps us to focus our attention on our emotions.

Start by thinking back to a time when you felt slightly anxious. Think of something that only was a little bit uncomfortable, like going to a new group or meeting someone new. Try to remember all of the aspects of what it felt like. Think about how your body felt, what was going through your mind, and what you wanted to do.

As you begin to remember those feelings, you can say to yourself: "This is my anxious pattern." Notice how you can observe and label it. You might say, "This is me experiencing anxiety" or "This is me with anxiety passing through me."

We call this emotion labeling. Naming an emotion helps us become calm and less tangled with the emotion, less controlled by it, or less reactive toward it.

Process.

Remember to use a soothing voice when you label your emotion. The intention is to gently notice their existence, not to immediately get rid of them. As you name these emotions, try to do it with compassionate recognition.

Discuss difficulties, challenges, and anything else participants notices. You might want to remind group members:

Emotions can be quickly and intensely triggered. It can be unhelpful to let your emotions dictate your immediate reactions. By becoming mindful, we become aware of what's going on inside of us—we take an observer's perspective.

When you cat mindfully, you can decide how you actually want to act. You become a wise actor rather than a reactor.

Emotions Running the Show

Through practice, we can learn to make emotions have less control over us. We can choose to act how we want to act rather than have our emotions force us to act. For example, we may choose to get out of bed even though we are feeling depressed.

Think of some times that you have let your emotions run the show. Now, think of times that you have acted the way you wanted and not let your emotions run the show. How do these experiences differ?

Process. Maybe share an example from your own life to get the process started if needed. If group members do not provide any examples, the following are some examples you could use:

Here are some examples of letting emotions run the show:

1. *Julio wakes up quite happy. However, he spills coffee all over his shirt during breakfast. He becomes very angry and keeps thinking about his ruined shirt throughout the day. He keeps feeling anger each time he thinks about it, which ends up affecting his behavior the rest of the day.*

Here are some examples of not *letting emotions run the show:*

2. *Sam is about to meet with his treatment team, and his body is feeling anxious. He is aware of the anxiety arising in him but also sticks to his intention of going to the meeting because he wants to ask for a medication change. He notices and labels his anxiety, does some soothing rhythm-breathing to calm himself, and does not let his emotions control him.*
3. *Suzanna had an argument with her mother and feels sad. She directs her attention to her sad thoughts and actions. Rather than letting sadness run the show, she tries to be more compassionate toward herself. Suzanna remembers her compassionate wisdom that she has a tricky brain and practices soothing rhythm-breathing to feel better.*

Body Posture, Facial Expression, and Voice Tone

(This part can be abbreviated or broken up as needed.)

Let's experiment for a minute with how our body posture, facial expression, and voice tone can affect our emotions. Let your body curl inward and drop forward in a depressed posture. Then, think to yourself, "No, I can't." What does that feel like?

Process.

If we learn to become mindful of our posture, we can become aware when we are holding our bodies in a way that makes us more likely to stay stuck in the threat system. So, we can, on purpose, switch to a more helpful or soothing posture. Now sit upright as if you're very confident, with your shoulders back in line with your hips, open up your chest, and lift your head up. Notice how different this feels.

Process.

> *Next, let's focus on your facial expression. Begin to smile gently, creating a friendly facial expression. Imagine that you are with a friend and are happy to see them. What does that feel like?*

Process.

> *Now let's experiment with voice tone. Say "mind slowing down, body slowing down" with an anxious tone. Then try saying "mind slowing down, body slowing down" in an angry tone. Lastly, try saying "mind slowing down, body slowing down" in a depressed tone. Notice how your body feels when you use these different voice tones. How we speak has an impact on how we feel.*

Process.

> *When we first try using a compassionate posture, facial expression, and friendly tone, it can feel strange and artificial. However, the more we practice, the better we get and the more natural it will feel. The subtle changes impact the way that we relate to ourselves and the way we relate to the world around us.*

Process.

> *As we try to be more compassionate in this group, it is important to be mindful of body posture, facial expression, and voice tone.*

Module 4

Feeling Safe and Receiving Compassion from Others

General Principle: Many of the imagery exercises can be quite emotional for some. Keep this in mind and explore emotions that may arise. It is important to explain imagery as concretely as possible. Draw on groups you have already led and describe imagery as a vehicle to activate the soothing system. Try different things to make imagery accessible for people who might struggle to think abstractly. Again, it is important to check in with those who are not keeping up. Drawing examples and explanation form group members who are following along will be most helpful.

Aims:

- Help group members understand the difference between feeling safe and feeling threatened.
- Discuss the flows of compassion.
- Introduce imagery.
- Introduce receiving compassion from others; practice ideal compassionate other imagery.

Welcome, Soft Landing, and Personal Practice

Welcome participants to the group.

Soft Landing

To start today, we are going to begin with soothing rhythm-breathing. Remember, our aim is to slow down and activate our green circle. We also hope to remember our compassionate motivation.

First, go ahead and get comfortable in your chair. Place your feet flat on the floor and sit straight, with your shoulders back and chest open.

DOI: 10.4324/9781003607557-4

When you are comfortable, gently close your eyes. Or, if you prefer, just direct your gaze downward.

Now, slow down your breathing a little. Settle your mind and body.

Focus on your breathing. Feel the air come in through your nose, go down into your stomach, stay a short while, and then move back out through your nose. Notice how your stomach moves gently as you breathe in and out.

Now, let's move into our soothing rhythm-breathing. Try to maintain a smooth and steady rhythm. When you breathe out, let it be a gentle, smooth exhale rather than anything forced.

As you fall into a rhythm, notice and focus on what you feel. Notice a feeling of inner slowing with each out-breath. Each time you breathe out, say internally, in a friendly and supportive voice:

"Body slowing down." (Pause.)
"Mind slowing down." (Pause.)

When you say these words, say them slowly. Each word should take longer to say and eventually the three words should basically use up the five seconds.

Try to notice how your body responds as you slow your breathing. Notice any sensations of soothing, grounding, or calming.

Let's practice that for 1 minute. You can continue to count your breaths for yourself if that is helpful. Or just notice the experience of smooth and even breathing. (Pause for 1 minute.)

Now, if your mind is wandering, remember that is normal. Simply notice it happening and then gently guide your attention back to an awareness of your breath. Breathe steadily in and out; notice the flow of air coming in and out of your nose. Just gently observe, allowing things to be as they are. Feel your body slowing down and mind slowing down.

Create a gentle smile on your face—the kind of smile you have when you're meeting a friend. Briefly acknowledge the natural changes that this smile produces in your body. Don't push or force anything; just experience. Notice how this feels. Notice your posture, facial expression, and voice tone.

And now connect with your compassionate motivation and say to yourself, I am coming here today and over the next weeks in order to:

- *Develop compassion for myself.* (Pause.)
- *Increase compassion for others.* (Pause.)
- *Be open to compassion from others.* (Pause.)

Okay, start to let these thoughts and motivations go. Start to come back slowly into the room. Notice your body in the chair and feet on the ground. When you are ready, you can open your eyes.

Welcome [back] to Module 4.

Process.

Between-Session Practice Check-In

Check that group members were able to engage in between-session practice. Check in to see if any group members thought about or used and part of CFT outside of group. Help the group process their experience, both successes and resistances. You may decide to share a personal reflection on how you integrated ideas from the previous session into your own life.

Bridge and Forecast

Review key ideas from Module 3 (attention and mindfulness). Re-visit key ideas from Modules 1 and 2 if useful (tricky brain and three circles).

Last week we learned about attention and mindfulness. Attention works like a spotlight and keeping our spotlight on threats affects the way we live. We also get distracted, and our attention can bounce around. It really is so easy to get lost in our thoughts. This is not our fault, but rather this is what our minds do! Mindfulness helps redirect our attention and focus on our intentions. This helps us get out of autopilot mode and be wise in our actions.

The last few sessions we have talked about how our brains, emotions, and past experiences can affect our lives. You will remember that we all have emotions that help us to deal with threats, emotions that help us to go out and achieve, and another set of emotions that are linked to feeling safe, relaxed, and so forth. Compassion helps us learn to work with and balance these emotions. We've looked at how we can use our bodies and, more specifically, our posture and breathing to help us deal with difficult emotions.

Introduce key ideas of Module 4 (feeling safe and receiving compassion from others).

Today we are going to look at the idea of an inner safe place and what it means to feel safe in your environment versus feeling threatened in your environment. We'll do this through three exercises: first building a safe place within ourselves, then imagining an ideal compassionate other—a being that makes us feel safe, and finally experiencing what it would be like to be with this ideal compassionate other. In this way, even when our life experiences have made it hard to feel safe, we can create that safety within ourselves to tap into whenever we need it.

Feeling Threatened Versus Feeling Safe

Materials: Handout 4.1
Handout 4.2

Understanding Feelings of Safety vs. Threat

Have patients open to **Handout 4.1** so they can follow along with the following psychoeducation that will be provided.

One of the most important things we should experience when we are children is a feeling of being safe in the world versus feeling threatened. This develops early on in our relationships with the adults in our life. When caretakers are consistent, present, kind, and caring, we develop a sense of being safe. When caretakers are inconsistent, absent, harsh, or critical, then we become more likely to develop a sense of being threatened.

While we don't have control over how adults in our life treated up (remember your compassionate wisdom that we did not chose our environments), we do have a responsibility to figure out how to deal with the consequences of those experiences.

So let's talk about how feeling safe versus feeling threatened might look now.

In threat mode, we are looking to stop bad things from happening. Our attention is constantly on the lookout for the next possible threat. Sometimes this can be useful, but it can also be difficult. Think back to the three circles—feeling threatened is based in the red circle, which is our threat system. What are the purposes of threat emotions?

Process.

Contrast feeling threatened with feeling safe. When we feel safe, we can relax and enjoy our surroundings, take pleasure from where we are, and begin to explore and try new things out. We can be playful and curious. Feeling safe is in the green circle, which is our soothing emotion system. What are some benefits to being in a soothing state? What does it allow us to do?

Process.

Let's look at examples to help us understand both threat and safety. Imagine a bird on a lawn eating some bread. The bird constantly looks for potential threats, and if any threat is noticed, the bird flies away very quickly. Better safe than sorry! The bird is unlikely to savor and enjoy the bread because it is in threat mode. If the bird feels safe, it will be able to enjoy its food and will even be able to build a nest.

Another example is coming to this group. When you first arrived, you may have felt a sense of being threatened. For example, maybe you worried about whether you could trust the group leaders or other group members. Maybe you felt as though you could not share personal information, like the kinds of symptoms you experience, because people might judge you. Would anyone be willing to share any threat responses that they felt when they first came to group?

Process.

Hopefully over time, you can develop a sense of safety as you become settled and you get to know people better. Perhaps with a sense of safety, you can feel more comfortable here, begin making friends, or feel like you can trust certain people who work here. In what ways can your experience at [your treatment setting] change as you feel safer here?

Process.

Feeling safe is part of the healing process and helps us create an "inner secure base."

Exploring Threat

Now let's talk more about how we act differently when we feel threatened versus when we feel safe. We will first discuss threat strategies. These are the things you do to try to prevent bad things from happening.

For example, if you feel anxious that people will judge you in a negative way, you might withdraw from people to keep yourself safe from judgment—maybe you are quiet when around other people, or you avoid being around people altogether.

What are some things you do when you are under threat?

Process. Write the responses on the whiteboard.

Invite participants to think about whether they would want to change their threat strategies or whether the strategies are too difficult to let go.

For example, if someone says, "Well I tend not to leave my room much because that is the safest thing to do." You might ask, "Do you think you could carry a feeling of safety with you so you can go out more? What are the things you might be frightened of and how might you deal with those?"

Exploring Safety

> *Now let's turn to safety. First, think about times or places where you have felt safe? Why did you feel safe?*

Process.

> *How are some ways you know you are safe? How do you feel when you are safe?*

Process.

> *What would you need to feel safe enough to take risks and develop in the ways you want?*

Process.

Imagery

> *Imagery is another skill, like soothing rhythm-breathing, that we learn in this group. Imagery is one way we can learn to feel safe. Creating images or places in our minds that make us feel safe allow our bodies to feel safe, as well. This helps strengthen our soothing system—our green circle. Imagery allows us to create a feeling of safety, this allows us to feel compassion and calm.* (Further explain if necessary.)
>
> *One of the common concerns people have with imagery is that creating a clear picture in the mind is difficult. This is perfectly normal, and it's true that we rarely have clear pictures in our mind. Images tend to be more like fleeting impressions—a touch of color here, or a sense of something there. Oftentimes, intentionally imagining sounds or voices can be easier; especially imagining people speaking to us. The clarity of imagery is not as important as the act of trying to imagine. We aren't creating perfect photographs in the mind, just fleeting images. For example, imagine a bicycle.* (Pause.) *Imagine an elephant.* (Pause.) *Imagine what you had for breakfast.* (Pause.) *When I ask you to imagine*

these things, your mind flashes an image for each. The images do not need to be perfectly clear, just good enough to give a sense.

Like we've talked about before, the way we stimulate our mind impacts our body. Imagining delicious food when we're hungry causes us to salivate, even if the image isn't in perfect detail. We only need a few key details for imagery to create physical reactions.

Process.

So, let's try some imagery now that can help develop a sense of inner safety.

Safe Place Imagery Exercise

You may need to remind participants that with imagery exercises, it might be easy to focus on whether we are doing it "right" or "wrong." Ensure participants that as long as they are trying, there is not a right or wrong way to do these practices.

Let's begin by remembering the difference between feeling safe and feeling threatened. What are the key differences?

Process. Aim to help participants understand that feeling threatened is about protection and defense from harm whereas feeling safe is about freedom to explore.

In this exercise we be imagining a place where you feel safe. First, gently close your eyes or cast your gaze to the ground. Take up your compassionate body position. Put your shoulders back and open your chest. Curve your back and start to slow your breathing. Allow yourself to obtain a sense of grounding. Try to focus on having a friendly voice and facial expression. (Pause.)

When we do imagery, our minds tend to wander, and we get distracted by other things. When this happens, try to shine your mindfulness flashlight on it: notice you've gotten distracted. Then, bring yourself back to the words I'm saying, without giving yourself a hard time. You might need to do this more than once, and that's okay.

Now, when you're ready, see if you can bring to mind a place where you feel okay and comfortable. This is ideally a place where you can feel safe and calm. This doesn't need to be somewhere you've been before or even a real place. Be creative, if you like, and see what you can imagine—somewhere that feels safe . . . comfortable.

If this is difficult for you, simply think of a type of place you would like to be in. Start simple. This may be a new experience for you. (Pause.)

Remember that there is no right or wrong way of doing this. This is just a way of exploring our minds a bit to see what happens. If possible, see if you can engage with a sense of curiosity and even playfulness. Allow yourself to see what emerges. (Pause.)

Think about the following: Would you prefer a place that is inside or outside? What is the weather like? Is it night or day? Is the air around you warm or cold?

Now consider some details of your safe place. Are you in a forest, or by the sea, or up a mountain, or near a nice garden? What is the light like? Is it dark or sunny?

If you're indoors, ask yourself, are you there because that allows you to feel comfortable? As much as you can, allow this safe place to be a place that you are not trying to escape anything. And, if you're indoors because you're trying to escape, afraid of what's outside, there's nothing wrong with that. For this imagery, however, you might want to consider somewhere that feels safe without trying to escape, whether that's indoors or out.

Next, imagine the kind of sounds that might be around you. What do you hear in your place? The wind softly pushing the grass? Waves crashing? Crickets chirping? (Pause.)

Imagine other sensations as well. What are you walking on? If you are barefoot in your safe place, how does the ground feel beneath your feet? What might you want to touch or hold? (Pause.)

Notice if you can smell anything in your safe space. If you could smell something in this place, what would you like to smell? Is it the freshness of the air, the spray of the ocean, or the sweetness of flowers? Just take a moment and notice. (Pause.)

Now we are going to imagine our relationship to our safe place. Though it may seem strange, we will imagine what it's like to experience this safe place welcoming us.

For a moment imagine that everything around you welcomes you. You have created this image in your mind, so it's part of you. This place is connected to you.

Imagine that the place itself takes joy in you being here. For example, if there are clouds above you, they enjoy you being here. If there are trees around you, they take delight in you walking around seeing them. They make you feel welcomed. They make you feel that you belong.

Explore your feelings when you imagine this place is happy with you being there. Create a friendly and open facial expression as you imagine being welcomed. Allow yourself to have a soft smile of pleasure at being there. Remember the friendly voice tone that we practiced last week. (Pause.)

You may notice that as you think about doing things in your safe place, the place may change around you. This is normal and commonly happens. You don't have to hold on to only one image of this place if your mind wants it to change. Again, the idea is to allow your mind to explore because you feel safe. (Pause.)

Now slowly start letting that image fade, come back into the room, and notice how your body feels in your chair. When you are ready, open your eyes.

Process. Consider asking question about what might happen if group members were to bring people to their safe place. Who would they want or not want there? If they weren't alone, what would it be like to be alone? These types of questions can lead to important discovered about interpersonal fears. These things can be asked either during or after the exercise.

Turn to Handout 4.2 and write down features of our safe place. This will be helpful for when you practice their exercise again in the future. Remember you can practice this exercise on your own or with others. Keep in mind that your safe place can change if you think of one that better fits. As you practice the same imagery exercise, your place can become stronger and clearer.

Check-In

Don't worry if patients don't experience feelings of safety right away. Be prepared to address and explore various fears, blocks, and resistances that might come up. For many people in this population, imagining a safe place can be exceptionally difficult when few places in life have felt safe. If several members struggle with the exercise, consider writing on the board elements and aspects of safe places on the board. Have group members who were able to imagine a safe place share. Ask if those who struggled would consider borrowing come of these elements when creating their own safe place.

The Flows of Compassion

Materials: Handout 4.3
Handout 4.4

Draw *the flows of compassion* on the whiteboard: Refer participants to **Handout 4.3.**

> *Now we're going to connect feeling safe to compassion. There are three flows to compassion and each one is important. There is giving compassion to others, which is usually the easiest to experience; then we have receiving compassion from others; and then giving compassion to ourselves. We will be learning about each of these flows.*
>
> *For the rest of our session today, we're going to focus on receiving compassion from others. As we work to increase feelings of safety, it is easier to receive compassion from others.*

> **Note for the Group Leader**
>
> In the following exercise, you are going to guide people to imagine a relationship and inner conversations that they can bring to mind when they are struggling. This can be very helpful for some, but be aware of individuals who may experience auditory hallucinations. For these individuals' the abstract nature of imagery may be harder to grasp. This can be addressed with exploration and discussion in group.

Building an "Ideal Compassionate Other" Imagery Exercise

> *Next, we will try another imagery exercise. This time we will try to create an "ideal compassionate other." We already worked to create with a safe space, so this exercise will expand on a safe space by working to imagine a safe being. We will eventually imagine what it is like to receive compassion from this ideal compassionate other. Now let's start creating that image of a compassionate other. The ideal compassionate other is not necessarily a person. It could be an animal like a lion or*

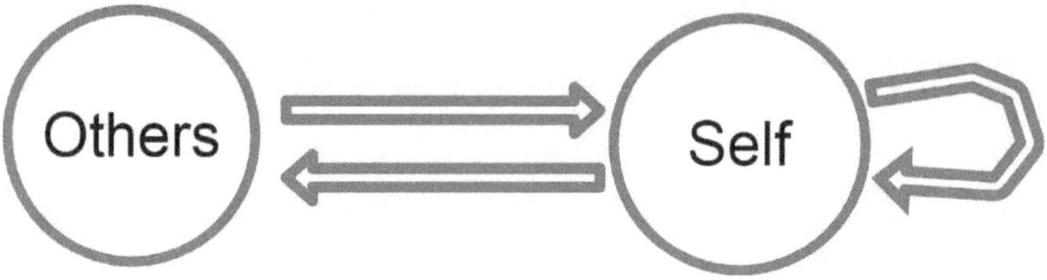

Figure 4.1 Flows of compassion

dog that protects, or it could be an object that is strong like a waterfall or tree. Whatever works for you is fine to start with.

Like with the safe space, this compassionate other can help us when we're feeling unsafe or stuck in our threat system. It helps us shift into a state of soothing and rest when that would be more helpful in the moment. The image of the compassionate other we create can lead our brains toward a compassionate way of being.

Go ahead and gently close your eyes or cast your gaze to the ground. We're going to start to imagine our ideal compassionate other. This compassionate other is wise, kind, helpful, insightful, and so on.

Ideal means that the compassionate other doesn't have to suffer from human fallibility, weakness, or bad habits. It is exactly what you would want, even if it's unrealistic. The act of creating this other is what is important for how our minds work.

Maybe start by thinking about appearance. As I said before, sometimes people prefer not to think about humans but may think of an animal or an object. The key to creating this compassionate other is that it has its own mind and that it completely understands what you are going through. It understands that we have tricky brains and that we can suffer and get caught in loops with our own minds. See what emerges for you. Just take a moment to consider the following:

- *Would you want your ideal compassionate other to have a gender? If so, what gender would you prefer?* (Pause.)
- *What is the age of your ideal compassionate other? Older? Younger? The same age?* (Pause.)
- *What sort of size would this ideal compassionate other be?* (Pause.)
- *Do you have any sense of facial expressions?* (Pause.)
- *Do you have an impression of hair color or eye color if they have hair or eyes? Remember you don't need to see anything clearly, just an impression.* (Pause.)
- *How might they be clothed?* (Pause.)

Next, we can start to think about how they communicate with you:

- *What sort of voice tone or sounds would you like for this compassionate other to have? Again, you do not need to have a clear picture of this. Allow a sense of this to be enough.* (Pause.)

There are many qualities you may want for your compassionate other. You may want your compassionate other to be patient. You may want them to be tolerant, wise, and friendly. Perhaps your compassionate other is gentle, open, and understanding. You can want a compassionate other with strength, determination, playfulness, and humor. Many people want a compassionate other that is easy to be with. Of course, there may be other qualities that you would like as well. Think of the qualities you would like yours to have. (Pause.)

Try to turn this image into one that you would like to be with and feel safe with. If you don't feel comfortable with the image, then play around with it. Play with it until it has the qualities you'd like so that you are comfortable with it.

Sometimes people want their image to have been through what they've been through and have wisdom and understanding from that. For example, a person who has dealt with depression may prefer a compassionate other that has dealt with depression like them. Therefore, this compassionate other understands them. It has wise and supportive advice. Your ideal compassionate other is close to you. It is understanding and shares wisdom with you; it knows who you are and what you've been through. Your compassionate other wants to address your suffering and help in any way it can. The ideal compassionate other certainly does not cause suffering in any way. Take a moment to really think about your compassionate other. Think of the characteristics it has. (Pause.)

Now, just slowly let that image fade away. Notice how your body feels in the chair right now and when you are ready open your eyes.

Process. Allow members to describe their compassionate other and write their responses on the board. Note how different but also similar people's images/figures are.

You can include **Handout 4.4** here and ask group members to record what they envisioned before discussing as a group. Because this imagery exercise may seem long for some group members, you may also suggest group members follow along and write down notes on their compassionate other in the Handout during the exercise. This may help some to pay better attention.

Check-In

If there are participants who still appear to be struggling to identify any aspects of an ideal compassionate other, consider collaboratively identifying and agreeing on some characteristics of an ideal compassionate other for the group. Those participants who struggled initially can then chose to draw on these group characteristics for the next imagery exercise.

Breathing and Compassion (Optional)

This optional exercise, provided at the end of the module, involves imagining breathing in compassion and breathing out threat emotions.

Receiving Compassion from Others: We Need Others and Others Need Us

Now let's talk about why allowing compassion from others is important. From the day we are born, we need others to feed us, comfort us, and care for us in order to survive—this is the way that our brains are set up. Our species would not survive otherwise. Being cared for has the same importance as food.

Process.

Help, care, and attention can be very soothing and, like we just talked about, are very much needed. Sadly, and tragically, we sometimes don't get the care or attention we need. This can leave us feeling angry, anxious, sad, or distrusting and causes us to pull for more support or to push people away. Our tricky brains can be uncomfortable with receiving compassion if we have not received or allowed ourselves to receive compassion from others in the past. This often happens when we spend a lot of time in the threat system and searching for safety. Again, this is not our fault, but it is our responsibility to learn how to respond to it. As we learn to accept compassion from others, we can begin to reclaim what nature has given us and we can feel more understood, less lonely, and less likely to rely only on ourselves for the support we all need.

Process.

Let's talk more about what receiving compassion from others looks like for you . . .

What is it like for you to seek compassion and help from others?

Process.

Who would you want to seek help from?

Process.

What are your fears of asking for help when you need it? What might get in the way?

Process.

Appreciation and Gratitude Exercise (Optional)

This optional exercise, provided at the end of the module, involves group members remembering a time where others helped them, reflecting on what that felt like, and exploring what they would like to say to that person.

Receiving Compassion from Our "Ideal Compassionate Other" Imagery Exercise

> **Note for the Group Leader**
>
> Provide group members with an overview of the following exercise. In this exercise, group members will be bringing to mind a "small life difficulty" and exploring how their ideal compassionate other can help them through it. The idea of a small life difficulty may be challenging for some group members to think of. Check in before the practice and provide some examples (e.g., waking up late and missing a class, having a friend not answer your call, staining your favorite shirt, etc.). As a group leader, providing your own small life difficulty will likely be helpful. Make sure patients have an idea of this going into the exercise so they don't get lost along the way.

We have created an image of an ideal compassionate other. Next, we are going to imagine relating to it. This is one more tool to help you feel safe when your sense of threat, the red circle, has gotten out of balance with the others. As always, during the exercise be open and curious.

To start, get comfortable in your chair, feet flat on the floor, sitting straight, shoulders back and chest open. If you are comfortable, gently close your eyes or, if you prefer, just direct your gaze downward. Go ahead and allow yourself to slow down your breathing for just a moment. (Pause.)

As we go through this exercise, go at your own pace. Approach this with curiosity. Try to notice what unfolds in your mind and body.

Notice what happens in your body and mind when you bring your image of your ideal compassionate other to mind. Obviously, this is going to be very different from if you bring to mind an image of someone who is critical of you. Remember, we're trying to create physical states that are helpful. We can use imagery to do that.

Sit with the image of your ideal compassionate other. Feel what it is like to have another who fully understands you. This ideal other wants to support and encourage you. As you get more comfortable with this imagery, you can then begin to bring this imagery to various life events.

For example, let's see how we can use this image with a small life difficulty you are dealing with. Don't think of anything too major. Just try to think of something that you are disappointed about. Or think about something that causes you some anxiety, irritation, or frustration. Bring this small life difficulty to mind. (Pause.)

Now imagine that you are with your ideal compassionate other. This compassionate other has wisdom, strength, and commitment. It has these qualities to help you. Remember the other qualities this ideal compassionate other has. You may want it to have patience, understanding, kindness, or an eagerness to help. How would you like your ideal compassionate other to relate to you with this life difficulty? Think about the following questions:

- *What voice tone would you hear?* (Pause.)
- *What would your ideal compassionate other say to you? What would it say of your strengths and struggles?* (Pause.)
- *Would it offer a listening ear or reassuring voice?* (Pause.)
- *Is it offering you a sense of being understood?* (Pause.)
- *How might it help you stand back and take a slower or more helpful perspective?* (Pause.)
- *How might it help you remember your own wisdom: that having difficulties is not your fault?* (Pause.)
- *What kind of things would you want to say to this image? Remembering that you can say anything you want about anything you want, what concerns would you like to share?* (Pause.)

Now slowly start letting that image fade. Start coming back into the room and noticing how your body feels in your chair. When you are ready, open your eyes.

Process. As always, pay attention to resistances and blocks.

In this module, we did three imagery exercises to help you feel safe: imagining a safe space, building a compassionate other, and experiencing that compassionate other as it understands and supports you through a difficulty in your life.

After you leave this group today, how might you use any of these three exercises on your own? Are there any situations where it would not be helpful to use them?

Process. Participants might suggest that these skills can be used to eliminate the sense of threat entirely. If this is the case, review the functions of each of the circles and discuss ways to use these exercises to find balance among the circles rather than never feeling under threat again.

Reviewing Compassion Process

Reminder

You can review the Jordan content from previous modules as needed, or you can go straight to the example from this module. Often a review is not necessary when time is short, and briefly apply the skills learned that day to Jordan's situation is sufficient.

Optional Review

Module 1: Dayroom fight, level drop, anger/anxiety, thinking loops; trick brain, "not my fault but my responsibility"
Module 2: Jordan's red circle scenario (anger); three circles, soothing rhythm-breathing
Module 3: Jordan's rumination on level drop, lingering anger; attention (flashlight), soothing rhythm-breathing

Now let's apply what we have been learning is this module to Jordan's situation. After Jordan's level was dropped, he worries he will get in trouble again. He finds himself focusing on potential threats. Any reactions from others make Jordan more upset than usual. After recognizing his emotions and realizing these worries are keeping him in the red circle, Jordan wants to feel safe. He remembers that he can use imagery to access a safe place. Jordan can also use imagery to increase his feeling of compassion from others. Jordan may think of an ideal compassionate other who understands how he is feeling and provides comfort. Jordan knows that the images in his mind may not be clear, and that's okay. As he uses imagery, he feels safe and supported. As he feels safe, he no longer focuses on potential threats. This helps him move out of the red circle and into the green circle.

Between-Session Practice

Review the benefits of imagery. Walk patients through one of the exercises within the module for the between-session practice:

- Safe Place Imagery Exercise
- Building an "Ideal Compassionate Other" Imagery Exercise
- Receiving Compassion from Our "Ideal Compassionate Other" Imagery Exercise

Safety vs. Threat

FEELING THREATENED

When we are focused on threat, we are looking to stop bad things from happening. This helps us survive, but constantly checking for threats can stop us from enjoying life.

Example: If a bird is constantly feeling threatened, it will fly away to stay safe, but it will have a hard time settling down to eat.

VS.

When we feel safe, we can explore our surroundings. We will have courage to even explore things we might fear or worry about. When we feel safe, we will also feel open to new experiences and will be able to grow.

Example: If a bird is able to feel safe, it will enjoy its food and will even have the freedom to build a nest.

FEELING SAFE

Handout 4.1 Safety vs. Threat

Your Safe Place

In the space below, write down features of your safe place

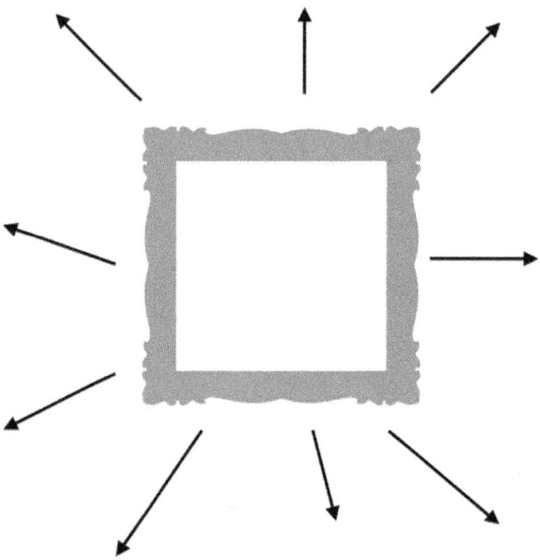

Handout 4.2 Your Safe Place

The Flows of Compassion

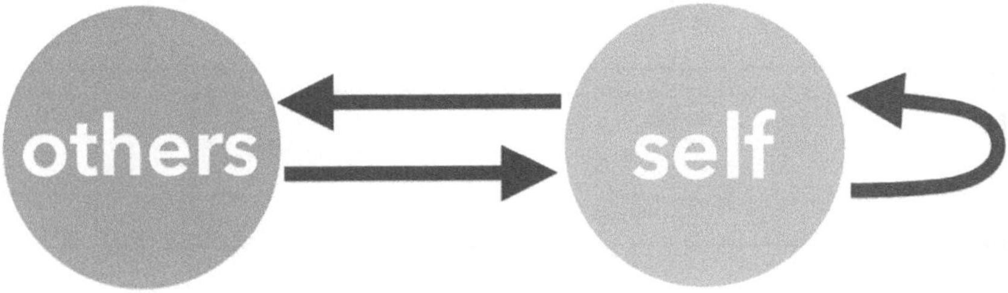

***Each flow is important. In this group we will be learning things we can do to increase each flow.**

Handout 4.3 The Flows of Compassion

Building the Compassionate Image

Here you can write down everything you would want from a compassionate other.

How would you like your ideal compassionate caring image to appear? They can be a human, an animal, or anything else you would like.
How does your ideal compassionate other sound (e.g., the volume and texture of their voice)?
What other qualities would you like them to have (e.g., thoughtful, understanding, funny)?
How would you like this compassionate image to treat you?
How would you treat your compassionate image?

Handout 4.4 Building the Compassionate Image

Optional Material

The Flows of Compassion: Breathing and Compassion

In this exercise we are going to try to focus on compassion as we breath. First, pay attention to your breathing. As you breathe in, imagine breathing in compassion. Imagine how this might look or feel. Next, try to imagine breathing out difficult threat emotions. Imagine how this might look or feel.

Take a moment to explore this.

Breathe in: compassion.

Breathe out: threat emotions (e.g., anxiety, fear, sadness, etc.).

Process.

The Flows of Compassion: Appreciation and Gratitude Exercise

One way for us to tune into compassion from others is to remember a time when others were helpful. Let's go ahead and think more about this. First, start my slowing your breath and move into your compassionate body posture. (Pause.)

Now, bring to mind somebody in your life who has been helpful . . . somebody for whom you have felt grateful. This might be a family member, a friend, a stranger, or a pet . . . Try to focus on the positive feelings of gratitude to the other person, no matter how small. (Pause.)

If you were able to talk with that person right now, what would you like to say? (Pause.)

If you were to write a letter to them, what would you want to write? (Pause.)

Process.

What was it like being able to accept care from this person? What made it difficult? What did you notice about your ability to accept care without feeling the need to repay?

Process.

Module 5

The Compassionate Self

REMEMBER: Do not sacrifice the moment for the manual. Be sure to assess and attend to diversity in terms of demographic as well as diagnoses within the group. Be aware of reasons for referral; this will inform fears, blocks, and resistances toward treatment that may arise throughout the duration of the group. This initial awareness of patient presentation and circumstance will allow the group leader(s) to better facilitate cohesion and participation.

Aims:

- Introduce, define, and practice self-compassion.
- Explore resistances, challenges, and difficulties related to self-compassion.
- Help group members develop a sense of their own compassionate self and how to cultivate it.

Welcome, Soft Landing, and Personal Practice

Welcome participants to the group.

Soft Landing

Start by closing your eyes and feel how you sit in your chair right now. Settle into your compassion posture with your back straight and shoulders in line with your hips. Remember, if you notice you're not paying attention to my voice or this practice, move your flashlight back onto your breathing. Getting distracted is a normal part of what our brain does. Noticing when this happens is mindfulness.

Now slow your breath. With each slower and deeper breath say, with a friendly internal tone, "mind slowing down" and then "body slowing down." Say these slowly. Alternate between the two phrases each time you breathe out—mind slowing down, body slowing down.

DOI: 10.4324/9781003607557-5

See if you can notice a sense of grounding—a sense of stilling and slowing, and also alertness. Notice yourself becoming more grounded.

Then start tuning in to your inner compassionate self. We bring to mind, attend to, and remember the wisdom that we have been developing in the course so far. We all find ourselves here with a very tricky brain and life experiences that have shaped how our minds and bodies work. This brain and these experiences shape the version of "us" that we are. We also have a mind that can learn how to change and make choices. We are developing the wisdom, strength, and commitment to help ourselves and others.

If you'd like to, you can try gently smiling. Notice the natural changes that this produces. You don't need to push or manipulate anything. Just experience what happens.

Now, briefly remind yourself of what we are trying to do. I am coming here today and over the next weeks in order to:

- *Develop compassion for myself.* (Pause.)
- *Increase compassion for others.* (Pause.)
- *Be open to compassion from others.* (Pause.)

Now allow yourself to let go of these motivations. Bring your attention to the sounds in the room, to how it feels to be sitting in your chair. And when you feel ready, open your eyes.

Process. How did you experience this practice?

Check-In

Remember to also solicit challenges, difficulties, or resistances. These exercises will not be easy or work well for everyone. Explore things that participants might find difficult (e.g., anxiety, boredom, confusion, etc.). Remind group member that mindfulness is like a muscle, you must work out regularly to see results. Activating your soothing system also takes practice.

Process. How did you experience this practice?

Between-Session Practice Check-In

Check that group members were able to engage in between-session practice. Check in to see if any group members thought about or used and part of CFT outside of group. Help the group process their experience, both successes and resistances. You may decide to share a personal reflection on how you integrated ideas from the previous session into your own life.

Bridge and Forecast

We've spent time in past sessions strengthening our ability to receive compassion from others, and we've used imagery to try to generate and strengthen this ability. Today we will attempt to generate and strengthen compassion in ourselves.

Compassion as a Brain Pattern

Activating the Compassionate Self

Invite participants to begin exploring the compassionate self by bringing to mind a memory of when they wanted to help somebody who was struggling. Invite them to close their eyes if they'd like. Guide them in this exercise with the following questions:

Bring to mind a time when you wanted to help someone who was struggling.
As you think back on this time, what were you paying attention to?
What were you thinking?
How did it feel in your body?
How did you want to act?
What did you notice in this exercise?

Process.

As you thought about these things, did anyone notice any of the three qualities of compassion (i.e., wisdom, strength, commitment)?

Highlight the intuitive wisdom the participants already have. You might connect this back to the idea that emotions are hardwired into our biology. A need to belong and connect with others is also hard-wired into our biology; therefore, we have all felt compassion before.

Compassion is one of various ways of living. We become better at being in a compassionate state through practice.

Compassion is like a muscle; we are all born with and have it, but it gets stronger and serves us better when we intentionally exercise. You might also think of compassion like riding a bike; in the beginning, it is hard, but eventually, with practice, it becomes easy.

Rember the definition of compassion: Compassion is sensitivity to suffering and distress in self and others, with a commitment to try to alleviate and present it. In summary, compassion is both doing good and avoiding harm. This also applies to being compassionate toward yourself.

Process.

> **Note for the Group Leader**
>
> There may be strong resistance toward the notion of self-compassion for some group members. Be aware of this and take time to process the psychoeducation presented. Self-criticism or self-harm are the opposite of self-compassion. You may need to explore the function of these things if they arise.

What do you think about becoming better at compassion through practice? Does this feel possible?

Process. Emphasize that the rest of the session will be exploring ways to practice being the compassionate self.

Getting to Know the Compassionate Self

Materials: Handout 5.1
Handout 5.2A
Handout 5.2B

Short Guidance

Think back on our first few sessions when we talked about how we didn't choose all of our environment or the body we were born into. Remember our discussion of how we did not choose the environment or body we were born into. If we had been born into a very different environment, we may be very different people. Consider how you act differently throughout the day based on your changing environment. Even small changes in the environment can lead us to act differently. Think about all of the emotions you've had over the last week. Was there a time, even a brief time, when you felt happy? Anxious? Sad? Scared? Peaceful?

The objective of this exercise is to notice that our state of being is constantly changing. Even if it feels like our life is filled with negative emotions, there are times when we experience other emotions and ways of being.

Given that we shift from one thing to another, let's reflect on things that can lead to these emotions—like watching a movie or hearing a story. These are largely entertaining because they cause us to feel something that we wouldn't have otherwise. Entertainment is an example of something that can shift our emotional state, even if it's just for a moment.

Can you think of what creates shifts, even briefly, in your own emotional experience?

Process.

Although outside factors can influence our emotional state, we can intentionally move the flashlight of our attention to focus on things that will help us to develop a more compassionate state. Focusing on things that make us feel compassionate, kind, and joyful can help us to develop this more compassionate mind. Remember our previous mindfulness practices where we moved the flashlight of our attention. We can move this flashlight whenever we want to help us focus on things that make us more compassionate.

Process.

Qualities of the Compassionate Self

Let's start by imagining a compassionate self. What would this be like? What qualities would it have?

Write the responses on the whiteboard. Use **Handout 5.1** to have participants write down qualities. Make sure to discuss core CFT characteristics if needed (i.e., wisdom, strength, and commitment). Make a note of what qualities were put on the board, as they can be referred to later.

Now that we have discussed the qualities of a compassionate self, let's try to step into it. Imagine that you are an actor that has been asked to play a very compassionate person. Try to become your ideal compassionate self the way that an actor would try to take on the characteristics of their role. Don't worry about doing this perfectly; just experiment with what it would be like to be your most compassionate self.

Process.

Note for the Group Leader

If the group has difficult staying with your during longer exercises, it might be more effective to treat the following exercise as an experiential exercise. You may wait for group members to answer each of the following questions one at a time and process answers as a group. This will give you a better indication as to which group members are able to envision and connect with a compassionate self and who is struggling to do so.

Activating the Compassionate Self Exercise

Let's start with grounding ourselves and getting into a physical state that more easily allows for compassion. Try to notice:

- *Feeling grounded; feeling heavier in the chair; sitting firm and stable, like a mountain*
- *Compassionate breathing that's slower and more open*
- *Compassionate posture, with shoulders back and back straight, relaxed but alert*
- *Compassionate facial expression and inner voice tone*

Remember, if you find yourself being distracted from these things or my voice, shine your flashlight back on them. This is mindfulness. If you feel comfortable doing so, you can close your eyes.

Now take a moment and try to step into your compassionate self.

What does it feel like to be that kind of compassionate person?
What kind of thoughts do you have?
What kind of behaviors?
What desires do you have?

Take a moment to really imagine what it would be like to be this compassionate self. If you notice that you're having difficulty, just notice this

> *difficulty, and then gently bring your attention back to what it would be like to be your perfectly compassionate self. See if you can feel it in your mind and your body. When you are ready, you may open your eyes.*

Pause and process. After addressing these questions, feelings, and any difficulties with the group, continue the exercise.

> *Now attend to the compassionate quality of wisdom—we have the wisdom that all of us have a tricky brain that we didn't choose. At times it can be chaotic, tricky, and painful—and this isn't our fault. This wisdom helps us understand ourselves and others.*
>
> *We also have the wisdom of how we've dealt with things in our life, and we have wisdom from natural compassion for those we care about that need help.*
>
> *Let's imagine waking up in the morning. What would it look like to have compassionate wisdom?*
>
> *Now attend to the compassionate quality of strength. As you ground yourself with your breathing, notice your sense of groundedness and strength. Notice how that feels in your body and your mind. You have the ability to feel stronger and more grounded.*
>
> *Let's imagine eating a meal. What would it look like to have compassionate strength?*
>
> *Now attend to the compassionate quality of commitment. See if you can feel committed to be compassionate. Do you wish to be somebody who is helpful to others and who would not carelessly or purposely harm them? Do you wish to be helpful to yourself and to not carelessly or purposely harm yourself?*
>
> *Let's imagine meeting someone new. What would it look like to have compassionate commitment?*
>
> *Notice how good it feels to be centered in this compassionate self. Try to picture what it would feel and look like in other scenarios if you could be like this. What would it look or feel like to sit or stand? What voice tones or facial expressions would there be? See if you can focus on your commitment to try being this way. Hold this in your mind for a few moments on your own.* (Pause.)
>
> *Now bring to mind someone that you care deeply about. Try to focus on that person and notice what wishes you have for them. Now take a moment to think of someone you've only briefly crossed paths with. Try to focus on this person for a moment. See if you can feel compassion toward them as well. Can you wish them well? Think about how you feel.* (Pause.)
>
> *When you feel ready, come back to the room.*

Process.

Highlight how spending time in the green circle allows us to more easily activate self-compassion.

Compassion for Others (Optional)

This optional exercise, provided at the end of the module, is about feeling compassion for someone that you do not like. This exercise might be helpful for group members who have great resistance toward compassion.

Compassionate Listening (Optional)

This optional exercise, provided at the end of the module, gives group members the chance to practice activating their compassionate self in pairs.

Compassionate Self Response

Have group members open to **Handout 5.2a.**

Now that we've practiced activating our compassionate self with someone else, let's practice applying it to our own lives. Think about a difficult situation, but nothing too major.

Wait until all group members have something in mind.

As best as you can, write some thoughts and that your "red circle" or "threat" self would have (for example, "I can't handle situations like this; I get too emotional," "I can never do anything right," etc.).

Pause.

Next, write down how your "red circle" self might act (for example, "yell at others," "avoid the situation and go to room," etc.).

Pause.

Last, write down some feelings as your "red circle" self when dealing with this difficult situation (for example, "angry," "sad," etc.).

Pause.

Have group members open to **Handout 5.2b.**

Next, let's change roles: activate your compassionate self . . . Change your body posture . . . Slow down your breathing . . . Remember all the traits of your compassionate self . . .

First, write down what thoughts your compassionate self would have during your difficult situation (for example, "I am trying my best," "This other person is having a hard time," etc.).

Pause.

Next, write down how your compassionate self might act (for example, "use a coping skill to feel better," "forgive the other person," etc.).

Pause.

Last, write down some feelings you might have as your "compassionate self" (for example, "calm," "grateful," "okay," etc.).

Process. Allow patients to fill out the worksheet in session, then share and discuss their response with each other. Emphasize how the compassionate self is a different state of being. Point out how the situation was the same, but our thoughts, actions, and feelings change depending on which version of our self we are accessing.

Reviewing Compassion Process

Reminder

You can review the Jordan content from previous modules as needed, or you can go straight to the example from this module. Often a review is not necessary when time is short, and briefly apply the skills learned that day to Jordan's situation is sufficient.

Optional Review

Module 1: Dayroom fight, level drop, anger/anxiety, thinking loops; trick brain, "not my fault but my responsibility"
Module 2: Jordan's red circle scenario (anger); three circles, soothing rhythm-breathing
Module 3: Jordan's rumination on level drop, lingering anger; attention (flashlight), soothing rhythm-breathing
Module 4: Jordan's continuing threat mode; feelings safe through secure place/compassionate other imagery

Now let's apply what we have learned in this module to Jordan's situation. Like us, Jordan already has some understanding of what compassion is. He can use that understanding to purposefully be compassionate. He knows that compassion is sensitivity to suffering and distress in self and others, with a commitment to try to alleviate and prevent it. Jordan is sensitive to his own suffering. He understands that having his level dropped has been hard. He also wants to help himself feel better. This is self-compassion. His wisdom, strength, and commitment all help him feel self-compassion. He has the wisdom that his brain was built to feel anger and that this is not his fault. Even though he knows it is not his fault, he has been trying to take responsibility for his anger. Jordan has the strength to notice his emotions and try to ground himself through mindfulness. He uses these skills to access compassion and balance his emotions. Even though it's hard, Jordan is committed to helping himself feel better. Jordan uses wisdom, strength, and commitment to have compassion for himself and live more intentionally.

Between-Session Practice

Today we will be working on one of the three flows of compassion. Do you remember the three flows? (Allow time to respond.) *This exercise is about self-compassion. We will also be thinking about the three qualities of compassion. Do you remember what those are?* (Allow time to respond.) *How might an exercise of self-compassion be helpful?* (Allow time to respond.)

Let's move into the exercise.

Refer to "Activating the Compassionate Self" exercise in the module.

Optional Materials

Training the Compassionate Self: Compassion for Others

Now take a moment to think of someone you don't like. Try to focus on this person for a moment. See if you can feel compassionate motivations toward them as well. Remember that compassion isn't about loving or even liking someone. It's simply about trying to understand and wishing them the best.

Can you wish them well? Notice what it's like to focus on these compassionate motivations with someone you don't like. It may feel difficult or even impossible—that's okay. Just notice what it's like trying to do this.

Process.

The Compassionate-Self

In the space below, write down qualities of your compassionate self

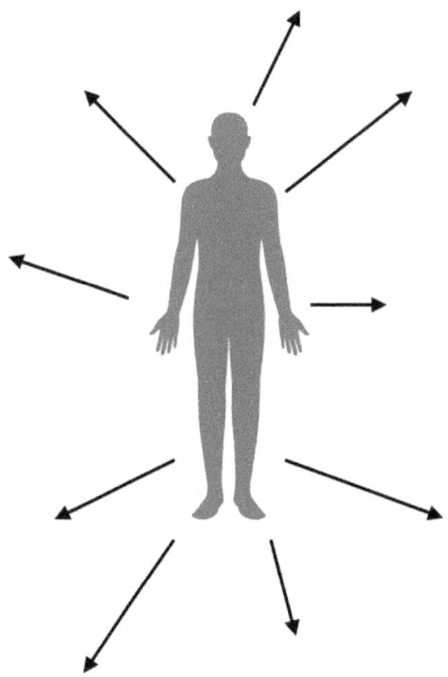

Handout 5.1 The Compassionate Self

A "Red Circle" Self Response

Think about a difficult situation, but nothing that causes too much distress. As best as you can, think about how your "red circle" self would react. After, we will compare the response to your compassionate-self.

My "red circle" self thinks: ______________________________________ ______________________________________ ______________________________________ ______________________________________
My "red circle" self does: ______________________________________ ______________________________________ ______________________________________ ______________________________________
How I feel (as my "red circle" self): ______________________________________ ______________________________________ ______________________________________ ______________________________________

Handout 5.2A A "Red Circle" Self Response

A Compassionate-Self Response

Think about a difficult situation, but nothing that causes too much distress. As best as you can, think about how your compassionate-self would react. Notice how different this response is compared to your "red-circle" self.

My compassionate-self thinks:

____

____

____

____

My compassionate-self does:

____

____

____

____

How I feel (as my compassionate-self):

____

____

____

____

Handout 5.2B A Compassionate Self Response

Explore how difficulties related to having compassion for others might connect to difficulties having compassion for oneself.

Training the Compassionate Self: Compassionate Listening

Short Guidance

Let's do a short activity working in pairs in which we practice activating and stepping into our compassionate self. Turn your seats to face each other.

Now in your pair, one of you can be Person A and one of you can be Person B.

Starting with Person A, each of you will speak for two minutes about a life difficulty. This should be something minor that you can talk about without too much stress. When I say go, Person A will talk for two minutes while person B listens without talking. When I say switch, Person B will talk for two minutes about their difficulty while Person A listens without talking. You can nod or use facial expressions as long as you do not talk.

Remember that it always helps us if we can ground ourselves and get into the green circle, so let yourself sit upright in your chair with your shoulders back slightly, open chest, shoulders over your hips, sitting with strength and authority. Step into your compassionate self as you listen to your partner share their life difficulty. Remember the intention to want to relieve suffering and be helpful where you can. Both the speaker and the listener are approaching this intentionally from their compassionate selves.

Process.

What was it like to listen to your partner while trying to be your compassionate self?

What was it like to talk with someone, knowing their compassionate intention?

Was it difficult to listen without responding?

Process.

Module 6

The Nature of Multiple Emotions and Finding Balance

REMEMBER: Do not sacrifice the moment for the manual. Be sure to assess and attend to diversity in terms of demographic as well as diagnoses within the group. Be aware of reasons for referral; this will inform fears, blocks, and resistances toward treatment that may arise throughout the duration of the group. This initial awareness of patient presentation and circumstance will allow the group leader(s) to better facilitate cohesion and participation.

Aims:

- Introduce group members to the concept of experiencing multiple emotions at once, with a particular focus on common threat-based emotions (anger, fear, and sadness).
- Help patients see how different emotions affect thoughts, body state, behavior, and memories, and that there are specific ways of settling for specific states.
- Discuss how multiple emotional states can set up conflicting processes in the brain.
- Discuss how the compassionate self can allow us to balance different emotions.

Welcome, Soft Landing, and Personal Practice

Welcome participants to the group.

> **Note for the Group Leader**
>
> The exercises introduced today may be quite emotional for some group members. We will be working with certain emotions individually as a way to differentiate and learn how they play out in

DOI: 10.4324/9781003607557-6

our bodies. By focusing on these emotions individually, we can help participants see the differences between them. Some group members may struggle with specific emotions, such as anger. It's important that if you start an exercise, you complete the exercise. Exercises may not be as helpful if patients are left in distress at the end of the group. Be sure to give time for group processing. If you find yourself explaining for long periods of time, you are probably doing too much.

You may notice that the experiential exercises need to be applied differently depending on the individual group members you are working with. Some of the interventions are much more powerful when they involve peers working with each other (e.g., describing emotional experience, sharing compassionate letter-writing, etc.). When you have a high-functioning group, this is how the intervention should be applied. You can adjust depending on the level of functioning of group members. If peer-to-peer interaction is not effective, you might model the experience with a group leader and co-leader. If group members do not seem to be understanding the experience based on modeling, you might move to a combination of high-functioning group members working together and group leaders/co-leaders working with individuals having difficulty. If this is not effective, try modeling with the leader and participant multiple times. The key is to be flexible and adapt the experience so participants understand, and more importantly, experience the function of the exercise.

Soft Landing

To start today we will begin with a soft landing. Let's practice the soothing rhythm-breathing exercise. This helps us become more familiar with how breathing affects the body.

Get comfortable in your chairs, feet flat on the floor, sitting straight, and lift your shoulders up a little so that your chest opens. Notice the curve in your back. When you are comfortable, gently close your eyes. Or, if you prefer, just direct your gaze downward.

Now, just breathe slightly slower and deeper than you would normally. Connect with your mind and body. Remember to pay attention to your body posture, facial expression, and voice tone.

Always respect the process and prepare your body. If you notice your mind wandering, point your flashlight back to what it is you want to pay attention to. This is mindfulness.

Now let's move into our soothing rhythm-breathing I will count you into this by saying: "In, 2, 3; out, 2, 3. In, 2, 3, 4; out 2, 3, 4. In, 2, 3, 4, 5; out, 2, 3, 4, 5." (Count about 1 second apart—remember to keep your counting steady.)

Develop a rhythm. Notice and focus on the feeling of inner slowing with each out-breath.

Say on each alternate out-breath in a friendly and supportive voice:

"Body slowing down."
"Mind slowing down."

When you say these words, say them slowly. So each word should take longer to say—and the three words should basically use up the five seconds.

Let's practice that for 1 minute. You can continue to count for yourself if that is helpful or just notice the experience of smooth and even breathing in and breathing out. (1 minute.)

Now it is perfectly okay for your mind to wander. Simply notice it happening and then gently guide your attention back to an awareness of your body. Breathe steadily in and out; just notice the flow of air coming in and out of your nose. Gently observe and allow things to be as they are. Feel your body slowing down and your mind slowing down.

Tune into your inner compassion—attend to and remember the wisdom that you have been developing in the group so far. We all find ourselves here with a very tricky brain and life experiences that have shaped how our minds and bodies work. But we can learn how to change, and we can make choices to develop the strength, authority, and commitment to help ourselves and others deal with life and inner difficulties.

And now connecting with that deep compassionate motivation, repeat the following to yourself internally:

I am coming here today and over the next weeks in order to:

- *Develop compassion for myself.* (Pause.)
- *Increase compassion for others.* (Pause.)
- *Be open to compassion from others.* (Pause.)

Okay, now start to let these thoughts and motivations go. Start to come back slowly into the room. Notice your bodies in the chair and feet on the ground. When you are ready, you can open your eyes.

Process.

Between-Session Practice Check-In

Check that group members were able to engage in between-session practice. Check in to see if any group members thought about or used and part of CFT outside of group. Help the group process their experience, both successes and resistances. You may decide to share a personal reflection on how you integrated ideas from the previous session into your own life.

Bridge and Forecast

Today we're going to be taking a closer look at some of our threat (or red circle) emotions. We're going to focus on threat emotions because they tend to cause difficulty. We'll especially focus on anxiety, anger, and sadness and how they interact with one another. We'll also talk about how we can engage the compassionate self in the interaction of these emotions. We will do this by exploring how we can experience multiple emotions at once, and be impacted in different ways by them.

Understanding Emotional Overlap

Materials: Handout 6.1

To help us to explore our multiple emotions, we're going to think of an argument you had with somebody. Ideally, this would be a mild argument, just enough to give you an indication of how different feelings and emotions can arise within us. This could be an argument with a family member, friend, peer, staff member, etc. Take a moment and bring to mind an argument you've had. (Pause.)

Have patients open up to **Handout 6.1**.

Instruct patients to break into pairs. When everyone has a partner, instruct the group to tell each partner about the recent argument. After a minute or two, have the pairs switch and the one who has not shared will talk about their argument. Once everyone has shared with a partner, ask the group:

What emotions were present?

Write these responses on the whiteboard.

Help participants process the idea of multiple emotions. Consider using the following questions:

- *Which emotion usually came first? Which one(s) followed?*
- *Is there a red circle emotion that you would rather feel compared to the others?*
- *Is there a red circle emotion that you really don't like and try to avoid?*
- *In your opinion, why do you think you have different emotions?*

Process.

> *Each emotion serves a purpose and has its own desire and motivation. For example, anger may want to defend one's reputation or character. Threat emotions are often based on some kind of self-protection. Fear, for example, may be monitoring for threats and ruminating on past threats or mistakes in an attempt to protect. Although "red circle" emotions can feel unpleasant, they have their own reasons for existing.*

Multiple Emotions

Materials: Handout 6.2

> *Let's further explore differences between emotions. Let's also explore how threat emotions are different from the compassionate self.*

Multiple Emotions Exercise

Have group members turn to **Handouts 6.2**. As a group, you will talk about emotions as an **observer** reflecting on the experience. You might refer to previous knowledge on mindfulness (a.k.a. attention as a flashlight). You may find it helpful to project, write the handout on the board, or use a poster-size handout to walk through the exercise with participants.

> **Note for the Group Leader**
>
> For exercises like this, it's very helpful to have a personal example you're willing to share. You should use your own example to model, particularly if it's difficult for group members to come up with their own. Additionally, this activity may be modeled with the group leader and a co-leader. Participants could watch as the leader helps the co-leader move through the components of a specific emotion on the handout. If the group is more symptomatic or lower-functioning, you may want to

break the group down to an experience for each patient, walking each patient through the worksheet individually. The hope is to be able to work through multiple emotions, even if they're listed as optional.

If you look at Handout 6.2, you will see there are four boxes. In this handout, we are going to explore our different threat emotions and how they impact us. Any questions? (Field any questions.)

Right now, we're going to try to slow everything down and look at our mental states in a bit more detail. Doing this allows us to learn about them and therefore how to work with them. We have many different types of emotions, but right now we're going to look at the three major threat-based emotions, then talk about how our compassionate self can help us with them. Each threat emotion serves a purpose. Anger is linked to a sense of having been wronged or attacked. Fear is linked to threat and vulnerability. Finally, sadness is linked to loss. We call these the "big three" because these are emotions that are usually impact our mental health the most.

We're going to explore these emotions one at a time.

To help us examine these different threat-based patterns, bring to mind again the mild argument we talked about earlier. The idea is to simply get a sense of how different patterns arise in us and how they work. We can refer to Handout 6.2 as we cover this together. I will also write information from the worksheet on the whiteboard.

Again, walking through each of these categories with a co-leader will likely help patients understand how to complete the worksheet for themselves. Doing this while writing co-leader responses will be additionally helpful.

Anger

Now you're going to go through looking at the different motives, thoughts, body changes, actions, and memories for anger. Depending on time, you may not be able to cover anxiety or sadness.

Bring an argument to mind and allow your mind to go over what was said, how it was said, and what you were feeling, thinking, and wanting to do. Remember not to get into your anger too deeply at this point. (Pause.)

Okay. Now let's see if we can explore the different aspects of anger. So, let's begin by looking at motives. We can do this by thinking of the wants and wishes behind anger.

Motives:

- *What has triggered your anger?*
- *What do you want when you're angry?*
- *What would be a good outcome for anger?*
- *What is the function or the point and purpose of your anger?*
- *What do we feel would happen if we didn't have anger or express anger?*

Process. While participants are writing their own responses, you will be writing participants' responses on a whiteboard that will help participants see the human commonalities of anger and that anger typically has similar motives. Help participants see that emotions are driven by motives. Find a motive and you find your source of threat as we often say.

Thoughts:

- *What are the thoughts that are going through your mind when you are angry?*

Encourage the group to allow anger thoughts to be uncensored. It is possible that individuals are having quite aggressive thoughts and fantasies that they may not want to reveal. You may ask: *"Do you have any aggressive thoughts?"* You may also need to model that it is okay to be angry and that it is okay to use angry language. For example, you may say about the argument you have brought to mind, *"I'm so pissed off right now! Why the hell don't you ever listen to me!"* Help participants realize that when we get angry, the anger does not always think nice things in nice ways because that is not what anger is designed to do.

You are desensitizing people to the fear of acknowledging anger or shame they may have around their aggressive thoughts and feelings.

We will now focus on our body reactions which tend to be automatic.

Body state:

- *What happens in your body when the angry pattern turns up?*
- *Where is your feeling in your body?*
- *What is your facial expression like?*
- *What is your voice tone like?*
- *What is your angry body posture?*
- *If your anger was to build and build, how would that be? Where would it go in your body?*

Process. Help your participants recognize that the body is automatically preparing for action in defense. Sometimes body pains (neck pains, headaches, etc.) are the result of non-conscious anger.

Behaviors:

- *What does anger want you to do?*
- *If anger was in complete control and didn't care about the consequences, what would you do?*

> **Note for the Group Leader**
>
> If you have the time, and if anger seems to be a significant emotion experienced by many group members, it may be useful to dive further into behavior. Remember to normalize aggressive thoughts and fantasies. Understanding fantasies, even if they are things we would never do, helps us understand anger. You can also explore reasons that we do not act on our anger.

There are different types of behavior that we often see linked to anger. First, aggression may be acted out through shouting, pushing, smashing, or hitting. Other examples?

Process.

Second, anger may be acted out by avoiding or cutting off, where we simply turn away or leave the scene of the argument or whatever is causing the anger. How else might this be manifested?

Process.

A third response is passive aggression. Things like sulking, stonewalling, ghosting, and disengagement. Do you have any other examples of what this may look like?

Process.

All of these behaviors lead to unhealthy relationship patterns. The key here is being mindful and aware of the behaviors that are occurring. It is important to remember that anger is not all bad. Anger can lead to productive change if harnessed. We don't want our anger to help us improve our life; compassion can help us do this.

Memories:

- *What does the anger make you remember when reflecting on conflicts with others?*
- *What memories come to you when you are angry?*
- *What are the memories that you associate with feeling angry that are particularly powerful or important for you?*
- *How far do they go back in time? To childhood?*

Process. Help participants gain insight into the fact that almost every emotion has a history. Very few emotions are newly experienced. Some people have much more intense anger—or fear of anger responses than others because of their history.

This explanation helps people recognize automatic activation (body based and conditioned memories) that accompanies anger. Even if we feel very angry, we can become mindfully aware, learn to tolerate, and choose to behave in compassionate ways.

Settling:

- *How do you cope with anger?*
- *How do you settle when you're angry?*

Process. Help participants process ways they settle (e.g., go out for a walk, drink, get into fights, sulk, etc.). Help them distinguish between constructive ways of settling and destructive ways of settling (e.g., reflecting or talking it over with a friend, moving into compassionate self, taking a walk, allowing themselves time to calm down, etc. vs. self-harm, cutting, drinking, taking it out on somebody else, etc.).

> Wrapping up anger:
>
> *What do we feel would happen if we didn't have anger or express anger?*
>
> *So, let's look at our angry patterns: Anger gets triggered because of some kind of block to what we want. Threat can trigger anger when there is some kind of attack on us or something important to us. Anger triggers particular thoughts, and our body responds in a particular way and has specific action patterns, which come with memories that go way back. We may try to do all kinds of things that are both compassionate and not compassionate to try to help it to settle.*
>
> *Okay, now let's take a minute to relax. Take a slightly deeper breath or two and imagine yourselves just letting go of anger for now.*

Process. Sometimes it helps to have people actually stand up and move around for a few moments; even shake themselves a bit. Then refocus them on settling the body. Now you can move to anxiety (or other emotions) in exactly the same way.

Fear

> ***Bring an argument to mind and see if you can locate a part of yourself that was feeling fear. Try and focus on that fear emotion.***

Motives:

- *What has triggered your fear?*
- *What do you want when you're fearful?*
- *What would be a good outcome for fear?*
- *What is the function or the point and purpose of your fear?*
- *What do we feel would happen if we didn't have anger or express fear?*

Process.

Thoughts:

- *What are the thoughts that are going through your mind when you feel fear?*

Body state:

- *What happens in your body when you feel fear?*
- *Where is your feeling in your body?*
- *What is your facial expression like?*
- *What is your voice tone like?*
- *What is your fear body posture?*
- *If your fear was to build and build how would that be? Where would it go in your body?*

Process. Help your participants recognize that the body is automatically preparing for action in defense. This is normal. Help them recognize symptoms common with fear (e.g., racing heart, trembling, feeling sick, etc.). Whereas angry emotions tend to tighten up muscles, anxiousness tends to cause trembling and weakness.

Behavior:

- *What does fear want you to do?*
- *If fear was in complete control and didn't care about the consequences, what would you do?*

Process. Again, emphasize that sometimes we have fantasies of things, and even though we would never do them, it is useful to be aware of and gain insight into those fantasies.

There are some common types of behavior related to fear.

One is submissiveness, which is used in an effort to control any tension and conflict. This can lead to resentment. When people are in less powerful positions, they can be appeasing and submissive to the more powerful people. Sometimes people will even apologize for things that were not their fault because the fear of the other is so strong.

Process.

A second behavior is trying to escape and hide—sometimes just walking out or cutting off. This behavior of cut-off (and we saw it in anger too) is where we simply turn away and leave the scene of the argument or whatever is causing the problem.

Process.

A third response is freezing—this is where our minds get blocked, we clam up, and we cannot think of what to say/do. We can also have a feeling of self-consciousness or shame. We can worry about coming across as silly or not being valued because we are not able to say things clearly.

Process.

A fourth response is distraction, where we try to avoid feeling the fear too deeply. We might keep ourselves busy so we don't have to think about the emotion.

Process.

Memories:

- *What does the fear make you remember when reflecting on conflicts with others?*
- *What memories come to you when you are fearful?*
- *What are the memories that you associate with feeling fear that are particularly powerful or important for you?*
- *How far do they go back in time? To childhood?*

Process. Again, help participants understand that every emotion has a history and that very few emotions are newly experienced. People will have different memories, and different responses based on those memories.

Settling:

- *How do you cope with fear?*
- *How do you settle when you're fearful?*

Process. Help patients process and distinguish between helpful and unhelpful ways of settling.

Be aware of helpful and unhelpful ways of settling fear, such as talking to a friend, practicing assertiveness, going for a walk, or positive reframing. Some examples of destructive settling or unhelpful ways may be drinking, eating in uncontrolled ways, cutting, and so on.

Note for the Group Leader

Address leakage: Leakage is where you are working with one emotion and then another pattern turns up. This is likely to happen working with individuals with severe mental illness. For example, while talking through anger, a person begins to become anxious or cries (sadness). Here you may say, *"Is it okay if we stay with just anger for a bit?"* You might also ask, *"Does this often happen to you when you feel angry—fear turns up and you can't really focus on feeling angry?"* Your therapeutic tone and openness will be important for this exercise.

Sadness (Optional)

This optional section, provided at the end of the module, allows patients to explore their experiences with sadness.

Emotional Conflict (Optional)

This optional section, provided at the end of the module, helps patients explore how their emotions could be in conflict with each other.

Compassionate-Self Integration of Multiple Emotions

So far, we've learned that we have different emotions that arise when we have problems and conflicts. These are usually threat emotions and they can feel intense. Threat emotions can easily become overwhelming. Although threat emotion can have potential benefits, we don't want to become overwhelmed by them because they have drawbacks.

We need to tune in and find a part of ourselves that has the courage and wisdom to act in a way that we want. We do this by accessing our compassionate self. Using just anger or just fear may not be the wisest or most helpful approach in managing conflict or other problems.

In order to activate our compassionate self, let's walk through a quick soft landing.

> *Sit with your shoulders back, spine straight, and chest open. Remember your friendly facial expression and friendly inner voice tone as we do this exercise. Close your eyes if you feel comfortable doing so.*
>
> *First, bring your attention to your breathing. Notice the sensation of mind slowing down, body slowing down. Become more grounded in your chair and stable in the body. Remember your friendly facial expression and friendly internal voice tone.*
>
> *As you access your compassionate self, first remember your wisdom that we all happen to find ourselves here with tricky brains. We didn't design our brains that experience all kinds of emotions from our threat system. We also didn't choose the environments we grew up in or are in now. So many things are outside of our control. So much has happened that is not our fault. Although this is true, it is our responsibility to try as best we can to cultivate the help within us. This is what compassion does.*
>
> *The second key quality of compassion is inner strength. This comes partly from wisdom of understanding the nature of our brains and emotions. We all find ourselves here trying to do our best. Strength also comes from our posture, and our breathing, and grounding. So, compassion is wise, and it has a sense of strength. It is not weak.*
>
> *The third quality of compassion is commitment. And because of our commitment, we try to be as helpful, supportive, and kind as we can be when we encounter suffering, whether it be in ourselves or others. We are committed to relieving suffering in ourselves and others. By slowing down, connecting with our breathing, and grounding our body, we can reconnect with the compassionate qualities of strength, wisdom, and commitment.*
>
> *When you are ready slowly come back into the room.*

Now that we have accessed our compassionate self, let's think back to your argument and explore your compassionate self.

Motives, Thoughts, Etc. of the Compassionate Self

Materials: Handout 6.2
Handout 6.3

Keep using **Handout 6.2** and remind participants to keep in mind the same argument they used for the anger and fear portions of the worksheet.

Motives:

- *What does your compassionate self want?*
- *What would be a good outcome for the compassionate self?*
- *What is the function or the point and purpose of your compassionate self?*
- *What do we feel would happen if we didn't have the compassionate self?*

Process.

Thoughts:

- *What are the thoughts that are going through your mind when you are in touch with your compassionate self?*

Process.

> *Your compassionate self will connect you to your values and goals and especially the intention to be helpful rather than harmful. When you think about this argument, what is your actual long-term goal? What happens if you allow your compassionate self to lift attention beyond the immediate and take a wider view?*

Process. Sometimes people begin with a slight invalidation or justification—such as "The argument is not important" or "It's not my fault." What you are guiding them toward is for compassionate self to have a different perspective which will usually (in this case) involves empathy.

> *I wonder if your compassionate self might have thoughts about what might be happening in the mind of the other person. You might think "What would be motivating or causing them to act in the way that they are?" Now you may go back to anger and say, "Well, they are just stupid." So, you may need to push past this a little bit. Your compassionate self might think "Is this something that typically upsets them?" or "Are they stressed or going through tough times?" The compassionate self helps us to see the other person's perspective and have empathy. When we do this, we have more control over our threat emotions.*

Body State:

- *What happens in your body when you feel your compassionate self?*
- *Where is your feeling in your body?*

- *What is your facial expression like?*
- *What is your voice tone like?*
- *What is your compassionate body posture?*

Process. Help participants recognize that compassion produces very different physical feelings to anger, fear, and sadness.

Behavior:

- *What does the compassionate self want you to do?*
- *If compassion was in complete control and didn't care about the consequences, what would you do?*

Process. There are different types of compassion behavior. See if they can come up with a few. Maybe they have fantasies of being overly (unrealistically) calm. Check for unrealistic ideals that cannot be meet. Notice how problems in the emotions might relate to the motives. For example, a competitive motive to win and make the other back down or submit is in contrast to a compassionate motivation for seeking fair empathic resolution.

One aspect that can be crucial is to help people think about the impact their behavior has on others. Central to the notion of compassion is the ability to accept responsibility.

> *There a times when our compassionate self needs to act in such way that we need to leave unhealthy relationships. It is important to recognize that compassion is not giving into insensitive or abusive requests or putting up with insensitivity from the other. Compassion gives us the courage and wisdom to move on. Even though somebody cares deeply for another, the relationship is quite toxic, and it's time to separate and leave that relationship. Sometimes what holds people in toxic relationships is guilt. So compassionate self will help with that.*

Memories:

- *What does compassion make you remember when reflecting on conflicts with others?*
- *What memories come to you when you feel compassion?*
- *What are the memories that you associate with feeling compassion that are particularly powerful or important for you?*
- *How far do they go back in time? To childhood?*

Process.

Growth:

We have seen that it's so easy for other parts of ourselves, such as anger, fear, or sadness, to take over. So, we need to think about how we can help compassion itself grow to be there when we need it to be. We have the seeds of compassion within us. It is really just learning how to cultivate them. What would help you do this?

Process. You will have written examples of all the domains in your fourth box called "compassionate self." Summarize that the seeds of a compassionate self are within us, which can allow us to think, feel, and do things differently. But like a garden, whatever we wish to grow will need cultivation.

Compassionate View of Threat Emotions

We now need to see how the compassionate mind and self view the other emotions. Have group members turn to **Handout 6.3** to write things down as you discuss as a group.

So now that you have explored your compassionate self, you can see that your compassionate self has a different way of thinking about life difficulties compared to threat emotions. Next, we can look at how our compassionate self views these different emotions.

Using your compassionate self, what do you make of your anger? How might your compassionate self address your anger?

Process.

Next, let's use our compassionate self to address fear. Using your compassionate self, what do you think of your fear? What feelings do you have toward fear? How might you try to help with your fear using the compassionate self?

Process.

Last, let's look at sadness. Using your compassionate self how do you view of sadness? Using your compassionate self what are you thinking and feeling toward sadness? How might you try to help deal with sadness?

Process.

Point out two things. First, the compassionate self often acts like a parent in the sense that it does not fight with these other parts of the self but accepts them. In addition, it can understand the thoughts and wishes of these different parts without invalidating them. This is very important because the compassionate self allows for integration and balance of multiple emotions.

Reviewing Compassion Process

Reminder

You can review the Jordan content from previous modules as needed, or you can go straight to the example from this module. Often a review is not necessary when time is short, and briefly apply the skills learned that day to Jordan's situation is sufficient.

Optional Review

Module 1: Dayroom fight, level drop, anger/anxiety, thinking loops; trick brain, "not my fault but my responsibility"
Module 2: Jordan's red circle scenario (anger); three circles, soothing rhythm-breathing
Module 3: Jordan's rumination on level drop, lingering anger; attention (flashlight), soothing rhythm-breathing
Module 4: Jordan's continuing threat mode; feelings safe through secure place/compassionate other imagery
Module 5: Jordan intentionally shifts to compassion; self-compassion in action (wisdom, strength, commitment)

Now let's apply what we have learned today to Jordan's situation. Jordan felt many emotions when his level was dropped. He was angry with the staff, sad to be farther from discharge, and anxious he might get into trouble again. These are all "red circle" emotions, or threat emotions. These emotions want him to do different things. His anger makes him want to yell at the staff. His sadness makes him want to cry. His anxiety makes him want to stay in his room. With all these emotions, Jordan can feel overwhelmed. Jordan can use the compassionate self to help deal with his emotions. The compassionate self helps him acknowledge that each of his emotions are important. Through compassion, Jordan can value what his emotions are telling him without letting them take control.

Between-Session Practice

Compassionate Self for Emotional Growth Regulation and Integration

We've learned that we have different emotions that arise when we have problems and conflicts. These are usually threat emotions, and they can be quite intense. Threat emotions can pull us in a number of different directions. Often, we don't want any one of the threat emotions to run the show because, while they all have potential benefits, they also have significant drawbacks. So, we need to tune in and find a part of ourselves that has the courage and wisdom to act in a way that we want. Using just anger or just fear may not be the wisest or most helpful approach in managing conflict or other problems.

You can probably guess which part of ourselves we are going to try to access and see how this part thinks and wants to act—our compassionate self!

First, we need to activate our compassionate self. Sit with your shoulders back, spine straight, and chest open. Remember your friendly facial expression and friendly inner voice tone as we do this exercise. Please close your eyes if you feel comfortable doing so.

Now bring your attention to your breathing. Connect with your soothing rhythm-breathing. Notice the sensation of mind slowing down, body slowing down. Become more grounded and stable in the body. Remember your friendly facial expression and friendly voice tone.

So, remember your wisdom that we all happen to find ourselves here as a part of the flow of life, with our tricky brains. We didn't design the brains that we have that give rise to all kinds of emotions from our threat system. Nor did we choose the environments we grew up in, which shaped us for good and perhaps not so good. Therefore, so much has happened that is not our fault. But it is our responsibility to try as best we can to cultivate the help within us. And this is what compassion does.

So compassionate wisdom is understanding that we have all just arrived here with a difficult brain and life circumstances, which gives rise to suffering, and that is not our fault. We didn't choose it, and we may not want it. The question then becomes, how might we deal with it?

The second key quality is inner strength. And that comes partly from wisdom of understanding the nature of life and the flow of life. We all find ourselves here trying to do our best. And it also comes from our posture, and our breathing, and grounding. These all contribute to our strength as we become stable as a mountain. So, compassion is wise, and it has a sense of strength. It is not weak.

The third quality is commitment. Because of our wisdom, we know that we are all caught up in the cycle of life. Because of our strength, we engage with suffering as a part of the flow of life. And because of our commitment, we try to be as helpful, supportive, and kind as we can be when we encounter suffering, whether it be in ourselves or others. By slowing down, connecting with the breath, and grounding the body, we can reconnect with the compassionate qualities of strength, wisdom, and commitment.

Slowly come back into the room.

Optional Material

Multiple Emotions: Sadness

Now you're going to go through the same process in exactly the same way that you did for anger and fear looking at the different motives, thoughts, body changes, behaviors, memories, and settling processes but for sadness.

Note for the Group Leader

Sadness can be an extremely difficult emotion, and this may be why people tend to avoid it. As such, some participants are very fearful of allowing themselves to cry, even in grieving, because they feel so vulnerable. This is particularly true for participants who have had attachment difficulties and do not have a sense of a secure base. Address barriers and resistances as necessary.

Keep an ear open for a very common problem where participants confuse depression with sadness. Sadness is not depression. Sadness is a biological response; depression is a cluster of maladaptive emotions, thoughts, and behaviors that interfere with normal functioning. Depression is a description of the pattern of sadness and is a diagnosis. Sometimes participants will describe sadness as depression where they talk about feeling lost, empty, or hopeless. Help them recognize that they are bypassing sadness. Another giveaway that a person is in depression rather than sadness is that when they feel sad, they become self-critical. You can use the example of going to see a sad film which makes you cry. Maybe somebody dies at the end of the film, but we don't necessarily feel hopeless or pointless or become self-critical because of this. Embracing all the maladaptive aspects of sadness becomes depression. Clarify this distinction as part of this exercise.

Exploring Multiple Emotions

Think about a difficult situation, but nothing too distressing. Try to write all of the possible emotions that arise regarding the situation.

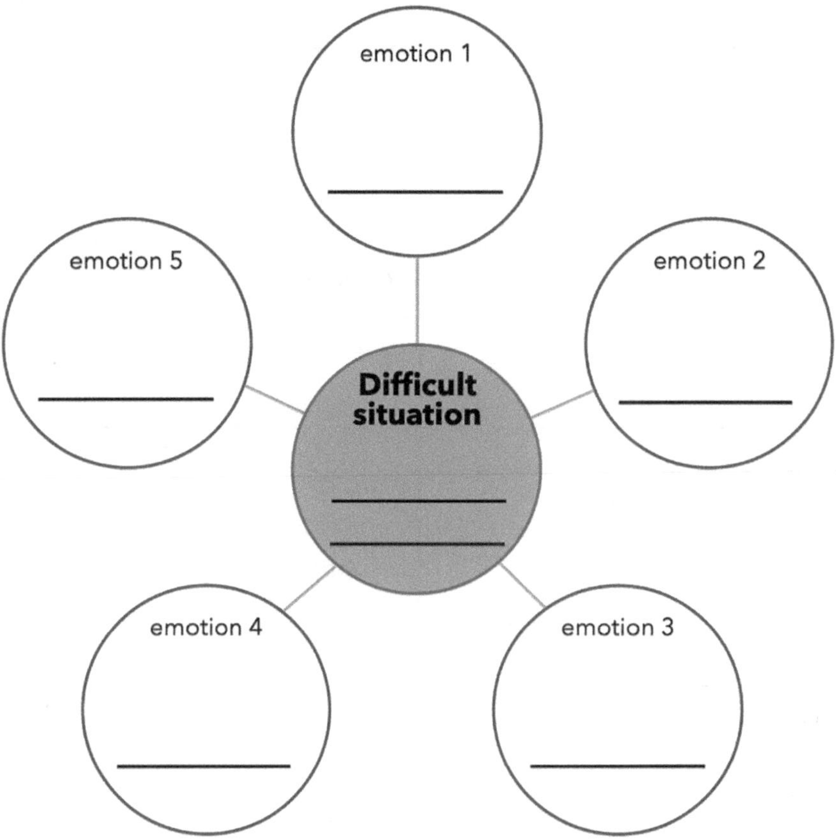

Handout 6.1 Exploring Multiple Emotions

Exploring Multiple Emotions in Detail

Anger	Fear
Motives: *Thoughts:* *Body:* *Behavior:* *Memories:* *Settle:*	*Motives:* *Thoughts:* *Body:* *Behavior:* *Memories:* *Settle:*
Sadness	**Compassionate-Self**
Motives: *Thoughts:* *Body:* *Behavior:* *Memories:* *Settle:*	*Motives:* *Thoughts:* *Body:* *Behavior:* *Memories:* *Growth:*

Handout 6.2 Exploring Multiple Emotions in Detail

Compassionate View of Threat Emotions

→ **ANGER**

How might your compassionate-self view your anger?

____

____

____

→ **FEAR**

How might your compassionate-self view your fear?

____

____

____

→ **SADNESS**

How might your compassionate-self view your sadness?

____

____

____

Handout 6.3 Compassionate View of Threat Emotions

Sadness can be a very difficult emotion. From an evolutionary perspective, when we cry, we can't see, we can't breathe very well, and we lose muscle tone. This makes us very vulnerable to any kind of external threat. From this position, it would be very difficult for us to defend ourselves and we might not even see threats coming. Sadness has been able to continue to be a part of our emotional system because there have been others around who have been able to support or keep us safe from danger.

Like other threat emotions, sadness has a purpose. Crying is very important for a lot of reasons! Crying releases tension in the body, and when we cry, we excrete various chemicals in our tears that sometimes can help us to overcome loss. On the other hand, repeatedly crying alone convinces us of how alone we feel. Continued crying by oneself is not helpful. Balance is important.

Process.

Let's explore sadness so we can understand how the emotion affects us.

Motives:

- *What does your sadness want?*
- *What would be a good outcome for sadness?*
- *What is the function or the point and purpose of your sadness?*
- *What do we feel would happen if we didn't have sadness?*

Process.

Thoughts:

- *What are the thoughts that are going through your mind when you are sad?*

Process.

Body State:

- *What happens in your body when you feel sad?*
- *Where is your feeling in your body?*
- *What is your facial expression like?*
- *What is your voice tone like?*
- *What is your sad body posture?*

Process this experience together. Write the responses on the whiteboard to help normalize participants' experiences.

Behavior:

- *What does sadness want you to do?*
- *If sadness was in complete control and didn't care about the consequences, what would you do?*

Process. Again, emphasize that sometimes we have fantasies of things we would never do. Help participants process through these. Discuss behaviors that are helpful and unhelpful.

> *There are different types of behavior we might see associated with sadness. We might start to cry or want to start to cry when we have a heart-sinking feeling. We know it is sadness because if a friend were to ask us what we are feeling, we might start to "fill up" or want to cry.*

Process.

> *Another behavior is withdrawing into oneself and closing down. We can kind of feel "frozen and switched off." You can tell when this is the case because individuals are more likely to have thoughts of hopelessness or self-criticism.*

Process.

> *Another behavior is feeling lost and going blank. This is not out of anxiety but rather just feeling lost and confused.*

Process.

> *Another is distraction where we try to avoid feeling sadness too deeply.*

Process.

Memories:

- *What does sadness make you remember when reflecting on conflicts with others?*
- *What memories come to you when you feel sad?*
- *What are the memories that you associate with feeling sadness that are particularly powerful or important for you?*
- *How far do they go back in time? To childhood?*

Process.

Settling:

- *How do you cope with sadness?*
- *How do you settle when you're sad?*

Process. Again, look for the usual helpful versus unhelpful coping behaviors. Explore the link between sadness and depression.

> *It's useful to distinguish between sadness and depression. Do you have any thoughts or ideas of how they are different?*

Process.

> *Let's explore what happens if you go to a sad movie and it makes you a little bit tearful—you connect to the characters. Does that sort of sadness make you feel hopeless or worthless?*

Process.

> *So, it is possible for us to feel sad and recognize that this might be different from feeling depressed. When we are depressed, we can actually lose our ability to feel sad and go very flat inside, with feelings of hopelessness and worthlessness. Depression is a different state from sadness. In fact, sometimes recovering from depression means we may need to recover our abilities to feel these different emotions, including anger and sadness.*

Process. Discuss with group the ideas presented and why sadness is important in spite of being potentially dangerous.

> *What would it be like if human beings never felt sad or cried? What would it be like if humans lost the ability to feel sad and cry? What kind of a world would that be? If people saw that you were hurt and they could be angry or even anxious, but they would never feel sad, what would that be like?*

Process.

Multiple Emotions: Emotional Conflict

> *We have discussed how we can feel different emotions in one moment. This is especially true of threat emotions. Even though feeling multiple emotions at once can be difficult, we feel each emotion for a reason and can learn how to find balance. We'll now see how emotions relate to each other—how they interact in our heads.*

> **Note for the Group Leader**
>
> This exercise requires more abstract cognition, as participants are asked to explore how different emotions interact with one another. This can be challenging or confusing for individual with certain mental health presentations. Forgo the section if unfit for your group.

What do you think anger thinks about fear?

Process.

When you are angry what would you like to do with fear?

Clarify that anger is always angry whatever the focus. You can also ask, *"When you are angry do you like fear? To what extent would you like to control anxiety?"*

Process. Write the responses on the whiteboard. Offer validation and invite curiosity and reflection.

What does anger think about sadness? What is anger's greatest fear/concern?

Process. Write the responses on the whiteboard.

So now what do you think fear thinks about anger? What does fear want from anger?

Process. Write up responses on the whiteboard.

What do you think sadness feels about fear and anger?

Process. Write up responses on the whiteboard.

Overall, our threat emotions do not always get along. These emotions can clash and lead us to be critical of ourselves. Compassion allows us to feel harmony between threat emotions.

Help and reflect on this new wisdom. Remind group members that they can now become more mindful that they feel different patterns of different emotions. Explore with them the possibility of continuing to have different emotions interact in the future.

Module 7

Self-Criticism

REMEMBER: **Do not sacrifice the moment for the manual.** Be sure to assess and attend to diversity in terms of demographic as well as diagnoses within the group. Be aware of reasons for referral; this will inform fears, blocks, and resistances toward treatment that may arise throughout the duration of the group. This initial awareness of patient presentation and circumstance will allow the group leader(s) to better facilitate cohesion and participation.

Aims:

- Normalize important functions of self-monitoring.
- Identify how self-monitoring can lead to a disappointment gap between the ideal compassionate self and actual self.
- Help participants understand the forms and functions of self-criticism.
- Explore fears associated with letting go of self-criticism.
- Explore the use of the compassionate self/mind to work with disappointments, self-criticism, and the criticized self.

Welcome, Soft Landing, and Personal Practice

Welcome participants to the group.

> **Note for the Group Leader**
>
> The experiential exercises introduced in this module can generate some emotions. Understanding and minimizing self-criticism is a core aim of CFT, so although potentially difficult, this module is very important. Appropriately sharing your own experience with self-criticism will aid in facilitating feelings of universality, as this is something all humans deal with.

DOI: 10.4324/9781003607557-7

Short Guidance Soft Landing

Let's take a moment to revisit our intention to develop our compassionate mind. We start by closing our eyes. We feel how we sit in our chairs right now. (Pause for 15 seconds.)

Settle into your compassion posture. Sit with your back straight and shoulders in line with your hips. Now slow your breathing. With each slower and deeper breath, say, slowly and with a friendly tone, "Mind slowing down" and then "Body slowing down." Alternate these phrases on each out-breath. Notice a sense of grounding with a sense of stilling and slowing. Remember to keep an alert mind. Notice yourself becoming more grounded. (Pause.)

Start tuning into your inner compassionate self. Bring to mind the wisdom that you have been developing in the course so far. We all just find ourselves here with a very tricky brain. We all have had certain life experiences that have shaped how our minds and bodies work. But we can learn how to change and make different choices. So, we are developing strength, authority, and commitment. We use these qualities to help ourselves and others to deal with life and inner difficulties.

So, as we are sitting here, we also say in a friendly and committed way:

I am coming here today and over the next weeks in order to:

- *Develop compassion for myself.* (Pause.)
- *Increase compassion for others.* (Pause.)
- *Be open to compassion from others.* (Pause.)

Okay, now just start to let these thoughts and motivations go. Start to come back slowly into the room. Notice your body in the chair and feet on the ground. When you are ready, you can open your eyes. Welcome back to group.

Process.

Between-Session Practice Check-In

Check that group members were able to engage in between-session practice. Check in to see if any group members thought about or used and part of CFT outside of group. Help the group process their experience, both successes and resistances. You may decide to share a personal reflection on how you integrated ideas from the previous session into your own life.

Bridge and Forecast

In this group, we have explored what it might be like to receive compassion from others and how to feel compassion for ourselves. We have also explored our multiple emotions, and have tried to understand them and give them space. We will now use the helpful qualities of our compassionate mind and self to deal with other emotional experiences that can be uncomfortable: disappointment and the shame that comes with self-criticism. Remember what the Stuart video taught us: our goal is not to make the inner critic go away, but to balance it.

> **Note for the Group Leader**
>
> If group members don't remember the Stuart video, it might be a good time to watch the video again at this time in order to review key concepts.

Process and Functions of Self-Monitoring

First, let's think about how and why we monitor ourselves. Anybody ever have a smoke alarm? What is a smoke alarm doing? Before it goes off, what is it doing?

Process.

Many systems that we use in everyday life are constantly monitoring how they are working. For example, your central heating monitors the temperature in the room and turns itself on and off according to that temperature. Smoke detectors are detecting smoke and then sounding an alarm. Systems monitor themselves because they have a function—to keep the system operating properly and efficiently.

Brains are essentially monitoring systems and the brain is similar to a thermostat. It is monitoring you and your body in very complex ways. For example, we can get into a car and use our brain to monitor our behavior as we steer, change gears, brake, drive in traffic, you name it! We are monitoring our behavior moment by moment when we drive. It's fantastic! No other animal can do that.

Inside of you, a monitoring system is always at work. Even while you're walking there is a part of you monitoring your balance so that you don't fall over. If you go for an interview or are meeting somebody new, then part of you will be automatically monitoring how you are doing and how well you are interacting.

We can monitor and then make judgments for all sorts of things, from memories to emotional states. For example, you might be monitoring what's happening in our group today, how therapy is going, how you're getting along with other group members, or whether you think other people are doing better than you. This is the way our brains operate. So, we can begin to look at a variety of monitoring patterns we engage in. The following are some of the things to focus on:

- *What are you monitoring?* (Pause.)
- *What are you focusing your attention on?* (Pause.)
- *Are you having any emotional reactions to what your attention is on?* (Pause.)

Process.

Along with this monitoring system comes an expectation or an idea-self. When you're walking, ideally you are not falling over. When you're at work, ideally, you are presenting yourself in a way you feel good about. A lot of the time, our actual-self doesn't align perfectly with our ideal-self. This difference between the two can be referred to as the "disappointment gap." What do you think that means?

Can you think of a time when that occurs or has occurred for you?

Process.

How do you feel when there is a gap between the person you want to be and the person that you are?

Process. Often people will share feelings of disappointment when considering this question.

What happens if you when you feel this way (e.g., disappointed)?

Process.

Monitoring systems can be set when we are very young. For example, suppose we have parents who are unpredictable and at times can be aggressive. How do you think that will affect our threat system monitoring programs?

Process.

> **Note for the Group Leader**
>
> Be sensitive to those with traumatic backgrounds when exploring questions associated with childhood. It might be helpful to explicitly ask how experiencing trauma early in life impacts how we monitor ourselves. It is recommended trauma only be directly approached in group if individuals are receiving additional trauma-focused psychotherapy outside of group. Group CFT can supplement trauma-therapy but is not sufficient on its own.

It's helpful to start noticing how we treat ourselves when things don't go right. One of the reasons for doing this is because the way we think and work with ourselves affects how we think and how our body feels.

Overall:

- *We constantly monitor what is happening inside of us and around us.*
- *This self-monitoring process is vital for self-regulation and social adaptation.*
- *While self-monitoring, we compare our thoughts, behaviors, and emotions to some standard or ideal.*
- *We self-monitor for a purpose; it serves a function.*
- *When there is a gap between our ideal and actual self this leads to self-criticism and self-correcting behaviors.*

Self-Monitoring Short Guidance (Optional)

This optional exercise (provided at the end of the module) invites participants to engage in an experiential exercise to introduce self-monitoring.

Functional Analysis of Self-Criticism

Materials: Handout 7.1
Handout 7.1B

We have talked a lot about safety in the past. We are working toward creating a sense of safety and then adding to this experience by imagining safe places and compassion from others. Ironically, many of us have developed a habit of creating safety for ourselves by being self-critical in an attempt to "solve" the disappointment gaps we experience.

We want to protect ourselves from danger or negative outcomes in life, so we try to use self-criticism to fix the things that we think are wrong with ourselves. For example, let's say that you were thinking that you would be discharged soon and were really excited about it, then you weren't discharged after all. You now have a disappointment gap, where your ideal self who was ready for discharge is different from your actual self, who is not getting discharged. To deal with this, you may become self-critical. You might start thinking about what you are doing wrong and have thoughts like "I'm so stupid, if I was better at participating in therapy then maybe I wouldn't be here anymore." Thoughts like these may feel safe because they seem to motivate us to do better, which can help us move toward our goals. For instance, if you were to have those self-critical thoughts about therapy, maybe they would make you want to participate in therapy more and then you could get discharged sooner. However, thoughts like these put us in the red circle (or the threat system) and actually make us feel worse.

Today, let's take a closer look at your self-critical voice and its role and function for you. We are going to explore how and why we criticize ourselves, see whether it is useful or not, and then see if switching to a more compassionate way of self-correcting or dealing with setbacks, failures, and disappointments would help us.

Imagine we could take away your self-criticism so that you'd never get angry with or beat yourself up in the future. What would be your greatest fears? What would you worry about if you didn't have your self-criticism anymore?

Process. It may be helpful to make a list of fears on the whiteboard.

Note typical fears of letting the inner critic go: I would become lazy, not learn from my mistakes, not develop, wouldn't see my flaws, or wouldn't care what people thought about me. Acknowledge how important these goals and values are.

One of the biggest blocks to giving up self-criticism is that therapists have not elicited its function or origin. Therefore, it is always important to see that fears of letting go of self-criticism are linked to perceived function.

There's nothing wrong with having goals and a desire to improve, and we aren't trying to change those goals. Instead, we want to see how our approach to motiving ourselves to improve can be more or less helpful. The way the inner critic functions when we struggle is often a problem. It's like the critic has a tantrum and is yelling at you, making it difficult to find a helpful solution. So, we want to find more helpful ways to motivate ourselves to improve.

Let's look more closely at your own self critic to understand it and its effects better.

Writing Exercise (Optional)

This optional exercise, provided at the end of the module, involves writing about and exploring the self-critic. It's useful for participants with adequate writing ability who struggle with the demands (e.g., attention, visualization) of imagery exercises.

Experiential Exercise (Understanding the Self-Critic)

> **Note for the Group Leader**
>
> You may choose to take group members through the whole exercise before they give feedback, as feedback on each set of questions can break up the flow. Of course, use clinical judgment and process when needed along the way if necessary. An alternative exercise to this is the previous optional writing exercise.

In the following exercise, we will invite you to take a deeper look into the process of self-criticism. We will try to see more clearly how self-criticism is operating. Go at your own pace with the intent to remain curious without pushing yourself too hard. Always keep in mind that what we're doing here will be a shared process. That is, we are doing this activity together and will be supporting each other and learning from each other.

So first, let's see what you think your self-criticism does for you. I am going to ask you some questions that you can just hold in your own mind for now. At the end of this exercise, we'll come back together and share our experiences and insights, then I will write them up on the board so that we can see what we have in common and where we're unique.

Before I ask the questions, let's slow our breathing just a bit. Sit upright in your chair, feet flat on the ground, and just breathe normally. With your attention on your breath, gradually slow your breathing. (Pause.) *When you are ready, bring to mind a small thing that you are critical of yourself about. Ideally this will be something you can talk about here with others—nothing too major. Just a typical situation that results in you being self-critical, frustrated, annoyed, or disappointed in yourself. Maybe bring a memory of self-criticism to mind to sense that feeling. Keep in mind that the idea is not to overwhelm yourself but to bring up just enough for you to work with.* (Pause.)

Okay, now that you are in touch with something that you feel self-critical about, imagine you can see the critical part of you as if it's outside looking back at you. Imagine you can take it out of your head and look at it. What form does it take? What sort of shape does it have? What colors do you associate with it? You might not see anything clearly but try to get a sense of it. Is it dark or light? Do you notice any textures? (Pause for about 15–20 seconds.)

Now let's see what this critical piece has to say. What is your critic actually saying to you? What words does it use toward you? What does it think about you? (Pause for about 15–20 seconds.)

Then, as you are looking at the self-critical part of you and hearing it say these things, what emotions is it directing at you? What does it feel about you? (Pause for about 15–20 seconds.)

Looking at your self-critical part, seeing its appearance, hearing what it says to you and says about you, notice its voice tone or sense of posture. What emotional voice tones does it have? What is its posture? (Pause for about 15–20 seconds.)

Now we come to an important part, which is the sense of action your critic wants from you. What do you think it wants you to do? (Pause for about 15–20 seconds.)

Allow this image to sit in your mind here for a moment. Then, at your own pace, start to bring yourself back into the room.

Process by using **Handout 7.1** and **Handout 7.1B. Handout 7.1B** is a filled-out example of **7.1**, to guide patients. Either have participants complete the worksheet on their own immediately after the experiential exercise or complete it as a group. In both situations, take time to write the responses on the whiteboard. Going step-by-step is important because it enables people to share their experience which in and of itself can be a desensitization process. Doing this step-by-step can also help participants gain insights into areas that they have been blind to. It can also be revelatory to see that self-critics tend to say the same sorts of things. Writing can also clearly reveal the hostility of self-critics. However, while doing this, write the phrases in a curious, non-judgmental way to create come detachment from the hostile messages.

Okay, so we've begun to have a sense of what form a critic takes when we imagine it.

- *What did your critic look like? What colors did it have? What shape did it have?* (Process.)

- *What did your critic say to you?* (Process.)
- *What voice tone did it take with you?* (Process.)

We know what it feels toward us, and we know what it wants to do. Now that we've explored this, how does this leave us feeling? How are you feeling about yourself right now? (Process.)

Let's explore the effects of the inner critic in more detail.

- *So how do you feel when you see this critic?* (Process.)
- *How do you feel when you hear what it is saying to you?* (Process.)
- *How do you feel when you hear the tone of voice it is using?* (Process.)
- *How do you feel when you consider the way it is saying what it is saying?* (Process.)
- *How surprised are you at what your critic is actually doing to you and the way it's doing it?* (Process.)

Process the whole experience. Perhaps, draw on the and explore the forms and functions of self-criticism identified at the beginning of the module. If group members don't seem surprised by their critic, it may be useful to talk about ways that we can become accustomed to things that are hurting us.

Even though we often think that our critical voice is there to help us, when we look more deeply, we can see it just makes us feel worse and undermines our confidence or sucks our energy. So how do you typically deal with how self-criticism makes you feel?

Process and explore patient coping efforts to deal with their own internal critical process.

It can be upsetting when we really listen to this stuff. So now let's ask ourselves: Does my critic really have my best interest at heart? Is it wise and does it know how to help, encourage, and support me? Is it helping me to achieve my goals—especially when times are hard? Does it offer clear insight for guidance?

Process.

What are some things the self-critic does that feel like it's helping but aren't actually that helpful?

Process. Some key information to highlight if it has not come up yet, it that the self-critic can be vicious. When this critic really gets going, it can tear us down. It also makes us less motivated to work toward our goals. It is actually undermining, not inspiring. Occasionally you will have some people who cling to the idea that the critic is good; these people may not have a hostile critic or may have been surrounding by highly critical people in their past, so criticism is something almost familiar/comfortable.

> *What ends up happening is that the self-critic causes us to be unhappy and actually less likely to reach our goals. Even if using this kind of threat and punishment seems to help, sooner or later we will get exhausted and disheartened. Not only that, but when we succeed, rather than feeling joy, we are more likely to just feel relief because our critic is quiet for a while.*
>
> *The tragedy of all of this is that there is a genuine desire in the self to improve and grow! But it is not necessary to be mean to ourselves in order to get better.*

Process. Help group members connect to the genuine intentions to succeed, noticing that they would prefer to be hardworking rather than lazy, enthusiastic rather than bored, helpful rather than unhelpful, etc.

> *In all, the intent of the self-critic is usually connected to very useful goals, such as goals to not be lazy or arrogant. However, the self-critics' methods of using fear and disappointment triggers the threat system that can launch attacks or avoidance. So, we are more likely to be successful by bringing other parts of ourselves into our awareness to encourage and support us rather than engage in the critical piece that tends to operate by fear, avoidance, and attacking. The compassionate self is the piece that will encourage and support our efforts!*

Choose one of the following exercises to practice responding to self-criticism with compassion:

Holding the Critic with the Compassionate Self (Optional)

This optional exercise (provided at the end of the module) involves exploring the self-critic as the compassionate self. It is a more advanced exercise, suited to participants who have done well with other imagery where complex emotions and experiences are personified (e.g., *relating to the ideal compassionate other*). It can be powerful for those who are experience hostility and anger toward their inner critic, allowing them to perceive it and its origins more compassionately.

Working on Internalization (Optional)

This optional exercise (provided at the end of the module) is to help patients think of a time where they think self-criticism developed. This is useful when participants have internalized the messages received from those around them (e.g., through bullying, messages from parents), and shifting into a less-degrading, more compassionate and wise perspective on these events.

Holding the Criticized Part of You with Compassionate Self (Optional)

This optional exercise (provided at the end of the module) involves imagining the compassionate self "holding" the self-critic or the part of them that is hurting. It is similar in function to *holding the critic with the compassionate self* but uses language that is more familiar to participants from other imagery exercises and soft landings. So, it tends to help people who strongly dislike their inner critic to adopt a more compassionate, understanding perspective.

Using the Compassionate Self

Materials: Handout 7.2
Handout 7.2B

When we suffer a setback or disappointment or make a mistake, we have two types of problems. One is disappointment in the thing itself, and the other is the attack (critic) we launch on ourselves. We may well be disappointed in our efforts or our behavior, but we can learn ways to deal compassionately with ourselves without treating the critical attacks as facts about who we are.

This awareness is powerful. In fact, one of the secrets to success and a happy life is the ability to fail compassionately. What do you think it means to "fail compassionately"?

This is really the ability to be disappointed and imperfect and fall short of our ideals without launching attacks on ourselves. We want to improve, of course, but the vehicle for this improvement is not self-attacking; it is self-compassion.

This applies to many things in life. For example, if you're learning to drive a car, the first thing is to know how to apply the brakes; if you're learning to swim or canoe, the first thing is to learn how to cope with going under the water; if you're doing judo, the first thing is to learn how to fall. Once we know how to deal compassionately with ourselves when things go wrong, we're not frightened of mistakes or failure. Then we're free to develop confidence and strengthen our skills. But if we always monitor ourselves and are frightened about making mistakes, then we will constantly be putting ourselves down which makes life more difficult.

Process. Have patients turn to **Handout 7.2.** Similar to 7.1B, **Handout 7.2B** is a completed example of Handout 7.2 to guide patients who might be struggling to understand the exercise.

Now, let's imagine our compassionate self.

- *What did your compassionate self look like? What colors did it have? What shape or texture did it have?* (Process.)
- *What did your compassionate self say to you?* (Process.)
- *What voice tone does it take with you?* (Process.)

We know what it feels toward us, and we know what it wants to do. Now that we've explored this, how does this leave us feeling? How are you feeling about yourself right now? (Process.)

Let's explore the effects of the compassionate self in more detail.

- *So how do you feel when you see your compassionate self?* (Process.)
- *How do you feel when you hear what it is saying to you?* (Process.)
- *How do you feel when you hear the tone of voice it is using?* (Process.)
- *How do you feel when you consider the way it is saying what it is saying?* (Process.)
- *How surprised are you at what your compassionate self is actually doing to you and the way it's doing it?* (Process.)

Two Schools Example

To offer more insight into the fact that we have these two very different styles of relating to ourselves, imagine you have a child you love, and you have a choice of two schools.

As you walk through the gates to one of the schools, you see a group of teachers that look a lot like your self-critics. (You can say, "So they look like big, tall, spiky monsters with snarling faces hanging around in the shadows," or whatever imagery people came up with.)

Process. Here you can circle back to whatever group members previously shared about their self-critic. Highlight that these teachers will feel the same emotions/thoughts for you that your critic felt for you.

They say that they will ensure your child learns because if your child makes mistakes, or is lazy, or is arrogant, in some way they will be critical and harsh. They will express their anger and contempt. They will ensure strong discipline and instill the fear of authority though punishment.

Process. Invite patients to think about what these compassionate teachers would look like and what their voice tone, posture, and so on would be.

So, you thank them very much, and then you walk to the other school, which is a school filled with compassionate education.

Consider their intentions and motives—what do they really want for your child what would make them happy? They might say, "Bring your child to our school because we are concerned with your child's well-being. We want to help them feel safe and then encourage them to learn and be enthusiastic about their abilities. When your child makes mistakes, we will support them so that they will learn from mistakes; we will encourage them to be open and seek help and be keen to learn how to be better. They will feel joy in trying to be the best they can—because it's important that children have enthusiasm to be the best they can. We want them to explore their abilities and talents and see where it takes them rather than be too frightened to try."

So which school do you want?

Process.

What stands out to you about the two schools? How would a person growing up in these two schools differ? How might the critical school and the compassionate school encourage students to put in their best effort? How would these schools help these children cope with setbacks? Deal with anxiety or depression? Deal with vulnerability?

Process. Review how self-criticism and the self-compassion differ.

Experiential Exercise—Using the Compassionate Self (Optional)

This optional exercise (provided at the end of the module) compares the compassionate self to the self-critic.

Reviewing Compassion Process

Reminder

You can review the Jordan content from previous modules as needed, or you can go straight to the example from this module. Often a review is not necessary when time is short, and briefly apply the skills learned that day to Jordan's situation is sufficient.

Optional Review

Module 1: Dayroom fight, level drop, anger/anxiety, thinking loops; trick brain, "not my fault but my responsibility"
Module 2: Jordan's red circle scenario (anger); three circles, soothing rhythm-breathing
Module 3: Jordan's rumination on level drop, lingering anger; attention (flashlight), soothing rhythm-breathing
Module 4: Jordan's continuing threat mode; feelings safe through secure place/compassionate other imagery
Module 5: Jordan intentionally shifts to compassion; self-compassion in action (wisdom, strength, commitment)
Module 6: Jordan's dayroom situation produces multiple emotions; compassionate self understands and balances emotions

Let's see how Jordan experienced the inner critic. When Jordan's level was dropped, he experienced self-critical thoughts. Jordan thinks about how he should have been able to show that the fight was not his fault. He thinks, "If I was better about explaining myself and proving that I didn't start the fight, I wouldn't have gotten in trouble. But because I am not good at communicating with others, I was blamed for something I didn't do. It's my fault. I'm so stupid." These self-critical thoughts are not helpful, and they make Jordan feel worse about himself. When Jordan listens to these thoughts, they add to feelings of anger, sadness, and other negative emotions. However, Jordan realizes that his inner critic is just trying to keep him safe and connected with others–it comes from his fear of being rejected. As Jordan pays attention to his inner critic, he also remembers his compassionate self. Self-compassion helps Jordan start to change his thoughts. He thinks, "It's too bad that I wasn't able to show the staff that the fight wasn't my fault. Maybe things would be better if I communicated better. But we all make mistakes. Next time, I'll see if I can stand up for myself more." Jordan sees how self-criticism and self-compassion are different. Compassion helps him learn from his mistakes without attacking himself. In other words, he is allowing himself to fail compassionately.

Between-Session Practice

Review **Handout 7.1** with the group members.

> *This exercise is meant to help us explore our self-critic. It helps us see that the self-critic is not kind to us. It does not have our best interests at heart.*

Compassion Takes the Lead

We are going to look some more at the critical self. Is the critical self helpful? (Allow time for responses.) *It may have helpful goals, but its methods of making us feel bad are not helpful. So, we aim to move away from self-criticism and toward self-compassion. Compassion allows us to learn from our mistakes without attacking ourselves.*

Take a moment to check your posture. Place your feet flat on the floor and open your back into an upright position. Slow your breathing for just a minute. Let's start to work with that pattern of ourselves that monitors us in a rather critical and sometimes hurtful way. See if the compassionate part and pattern within you can help it. First, we are giving space to engage our compassionate self. We slow the breathing a little, centering our awareness in the body, feeling grounded. We notice that we have our strength and wisdom and commitment to do this work.

Now imagine your critical self in front of you, being critical. You are watching it. Hold to your compassionate position; be your compassionate self. Now as you are observing the critical piece being critical, see if you can look behind the critic and see what's driving it. Can you see any fears? Rejection? Inferiority? Not being wanted? Consider the pains that brought that fear to life, like disappointments or what people may have said. Why is this self-criticism so harsh? Could it be sadness? Loss? What's behind this harsh attitude? Imagine your compassionate self is curious about the needs and fears of this self-critical part of you.

Holding our compassionate position, we now offer a compassionate wish. We wish that whatever is causing this desire to be critical may stop. We wish to find peace.

What compassionate message would you like to leave the critical self with? As your compassionate self, ask yourself these questions: What would you like to hear and to know? What would you need to feel peace?

You might offer messages to your critic such as:

- *I see you are frustrated and tired. However, the way you are trying to motivate me is not working. You can rest. I'm doing this job; I'm taking the lead. Thank you for trying.*

- *I know you are scared or angry, but you can feel safe now. I'm leading the change; everything will be smoother for all of us.*
- *May you feel safe and at peace.*

Slowly bring your attention back to the room as you are ready. Notice sounds; notice your body. Open your eyes.

Pause

When might this exercise be helpful? (Allow time for responses.)

Optional Material

Process and Functions of Self-Monitoring: Self-Monitoring Short Guidance

Invite group members to engage in an experiential exercise to introduce self-monitoring. Choose among the following examples or make up your own:

- Ask everyone to count backward by 7s from 1,000.
- Ask everybody to draw a picture of a face on the whiteboard.
- Ask participants to say something about how random words connect to themselves (e.g., *apple*, *milk*, *house*, *blue*, etc.).

Ask participants about what they were monitoring during the exercise, using the following questions:

Where was your attention during the activity?
What thoughts did you have about yourselves during the activity?

Functional Analysis of Self-Criticism: Writing Exercise

Process. The goal is to soften the inner critic. The critic keeps us in threat. Remind participants that we're not ever trying to get rid of the red circle.

Have notebook paper for each member and have them respond in writing to each of the following prompts. Process along the way.

- Think about a behavior you would like to change, something causing you difficulty that activated your inner critic. For example, "I procrastinate," "I don't exercise," "I get angry too easily," etc.
- Write down what you typically say to yourself when you find yourself doing (or not doing) this behavior. *What words does your critic use?*

Functional Analysis - Self-Criticism

Greatest fears:

Looks like:	**Says to me:**	**Feels about me:**	**Does to me:**

What I am now thinking and feeling about myself:

Handout 7.1A Functional Analysis of Self-Criticism

Functional Analysis - Self-Criticism

Worked Example

Greatest fears:

Become arrogant; hurt other people; go wild; never get anything done; embarrass myself; be lazy; be criticized by others; have no friends.

Looks like:	Says to me:	Feels about me:	Does to me:
Angry self; monster with big mouth and sharp teeth, a greenish slimy thing, black eyes, a big shadow; pointing finger.	You're pathetic; you always are a disappointment; you are a screw up; you aren't good; you're a coward; you're disgusting; if people really knew about you, they wouldn't like you.	Anger; disappointment; disgust; shame; rejection.	Shut me up; kick me; shake me to wake up; shout; give up on me.

What I am now thinking and feeling about myself:

Sadness; loneliness; anger; tiredness; exhausted; betrayed; depressed.

Handout 7.1B Functional Analysis of Self-Criticism (Worked Example)

Functional Analysis - Compassionate-Self

Greatest wishes for me:			
Looks like:	**Says to me:**	**Feels about me:**	**Does to/for me:**
What I am now thinking and feeling about myself:			

Handout 7.2A Functional Analysis of the Compassionate Self

Functional Analysis - Compassionate-Self

Worked Example

Greatest wishes for me:

Be less selfish; be true to myself; feel safe; be kind to myself and others; live a valued life; be humble; be helpful; have courage; keep going if it gets tough.

Looks like:	Says to me:	Feels about me:	Does to/for me:
Mother Earth; butterfly; angel; sunflower; sun.	Life is tricky; it's not your fault; let's see what we can do; it is okay; you are okay; this is disappointing but we can try again; you have a good heart.	Unconditional love; care; acceptance; connected; committed; trusting.	Be a support; just be there; hold my hand; act like a friend.

What I am now thinking and feeling about myself:

Light; hopeful; soothed; not judged; energized; accepted.

Handout 7.2B Functional Analysis of the Compassionate Self (Worked Example)

- Now notice and write down hoe you feel when you criticize yourself (e.g., defeated, helpless, shamed, etc.).
- Now try writing some words of compassion for yourself as a reaction to this criticism (a validating response, like "Wow, this hurts").
- Become curious about this inner critic. ***Why has the critic there? Is your inner critic trying to protect you in some way? Is it trying to meet some need?*** Compassionately acknowledge any fears or pain driving the critic. If you noticed a need, thank the critic for its intention. Often people acknowledge the critics efforts to notice and attend to values. The intention is good; however, the method it uses is not serving you well.
- Ask yourself: ***What if I had a friend with this struggle? What compassionate words would I share?***
- Giving space for that internal wisdom, your compassionate voice also sees how this behavior is getting in the way. It also wants you to change; it wants to support you in making a change. ***What is your compassionate voice telling you about changing?***

Functional Analysis of Self-Criticism: Holding the Critic with the Compassionate Self

> ***Let's now start to work with that part and pattern of ourselves that seems to be monitoring us in a rather critical and sometimes hurtful way and see if the compassionate part and pattern of ourselves can help it.***
>
> ***So first we are going to try to engage our compassionate self.*** (Pause for 30 seconds.)
>
> ***Now imagine your critical self in front of you being critical—but you are watching it—holding to your compassionate position.***
>
> ***Now as you are observing it doing its criticism—see if you can "look behind" the critic and see what's driving it. Can you see any fears—maybe fear of rejection or inferiority—not being wanted? It's a bit like the Wizard of Oz phenomenon of pulling back the curtains. Maybe even consider the hurts that brought it to life—the disappointments or what other people said. Remember, try as best you can not to be pulled into feeling those hurts and fears again because, as the compassionate self, you are being a witness to them.***

Process. Keep an eye on the degree to which people are getting pulled into feeling sad or reactivating memories that are painful for them. If you have group members with traumatic backgrounds, then you will need to prepare them for this. In addition, you may help them to touch on grief coming up. Make sure you help group members return to a good mental state before the session ends.

> ***Holding our compassionate position, we now offer a compassionate wish that "whatever is causing this desire to be critical of me—to say***

or feel those things toward me—may that cease, and you find peace from them."

Process. If group members say "I just want it to go away," "Tell it to stop hurting me," "Kill it," etc., then you can point out that this emotion might be anger. Then bring them back to the compassionate self.

> **Note for the Group Leader**
>
> If participants have identified their inner critical voice with the voice of someone in their life, normalize this as it is common critical voices around us become internalized. Let group members know that in a future module, we will be learning about and using forgiveness that may help with this type of inner critic. Suggest now that the compassionate self will always side with them.

It's important that the compassionate self tries to see the fear or hurt behind criticism—and the compassion goes to that fear, hurdle, or grief, not to the actual anger or contempt of the critic. What compassionate message would you like to leave the critical self with—what would you like it to hear and to know?

Process.

It's important that the compassionate self tries to see the fear or hurt behind criticism—and the compassion goes to that fear, hurdle, or grief not to the actual anger or contempt of the critic. What compassionate message would you like to leave the critical self with—what would you like it to hear and to know?

You'd like to see where this critical part of you is coming from, because you recognize it's really an echo or a memory of someone else who was hostile to you. It's not actually your voice. The issue is how you are going to recognize that you do not agree to continue to echo this in your head anymore because your compassionate self has wisdom and strength.

You will see that the compassionate self always respects the critic and tries to see the fear behind the critic. For example, Eleanor—who suffered from voices that were very hostile and persecutory—talks about how she learned to address these hostile voices with compassion and understanding.

Functional Analysis of Self-Criticism: Working on Internalization

> **Note for the Group Leader**
>
> Generally, people are able to see that they would not have chosen the self-critic, but would instead have chosen to be cared for. So again, you can point to the fact that this is wisdom. Highlight that all we learn in group expands our compassionate wisdom. The key always is to stop, slow down, be mindful, and switch to a compassionate self. The more you can practice this switch in session, the better, so you see more opportunities to say to the patients, "Okay, in this moment, what would your compassionate self say?" or "What would your compassion self think?"

In this exercise, you help patients think about how they've learned to internalize or echo certain ways of thinking about themselves that came from others. To start this exercise, help participants recall a point in their lives where they remember an event where they were criticized. You can ask them simply to sit quietly and bring to mind a particular time where they think their self-critic really developed. Suggest that this will likely be an event in childhood (e.g., bullying, disagreement with parents).

Hol the event in mind . . . What was happening? What was the disappointment or the threat? Can you notice how automatic the upset inside of you was and how the critic turned up then out of frustration or fear? What would you have needed in order not to have thought like that or taken on those self-judgments? If you have a child that you love, would you want them to take on or internalize those judgments? If you could have chosen how the parent or others at school behaved toward you, would you have chosen for them to act that way? What would you have chosen? If you'd had a compassionate mind on those days, how would you ideally like to have dealt with it?

So you have internal wisdom that this is not something that you would have chosen, and the reason that you were criticized in a hurtful and unhelpful way was something to do with the problems of the other person. This is an opportunity for you to begin to treat yourself with your own compassionate wisdom—to find your own inner voice and not rely on the judgments of others. Recognizing that your own inner voice has a lot of compassionate wisdom and strength and will guide you if you let it.

Process.

This can be a profound experience for some people. You might need to allot additional time to processing this exercise; it can unlock grief and pain. As always, circle back to compassion.

Functional Analysis of Self-Criticism: Holding the Criticized Part of You with Compassionate Self

In the module so far, we have seen that we have different ways of responding to setbacks and failures. Sometimes, maybe often, we respond with self-criticism. What we want to do here is figure out what to do about this critical part of ourselves. For the most part, simply arguing with it or fighting with it is not helpful because it is not addressing the underlying fears and worries that the critic is often sitting on and hiding from. So, we need to offer a compassionate mind to the critic.

First, let's get into our compassionate self, and slow the breath. If you are comfortable, close your eyes or direct your gaze downward. (Pause.) *And remember your commitment to try as best we can to be helpful rather than harmful—even to the parts of us that beat us up.* (Pause for 15 to 20 seconds.)

Now bring that critic to mind that you saw earlier. Out in front of you again, get a sense of its presence or form that it takes. Remind yourself of the kind of things it says, what it feels, and what it might want to do to you. Next, as the compassionate self, just observe it without engaging it for a moment. Imagine you can see behind it. Imagine you can see how it started up: What is its greatest fear? What hurt sits behind it? In other words, you aren't taking it at face value; you're seeing what triggered it, such as a disappointment or fear of rejection or something else.

If you're feeling lost or overwhelmed by the critic's attacks, then take a moment to redirect yourself to your breath, slowing it, following it in and out. (Allow time for this.) *When you feel grounded again, engage in a way where you can understand your critic. But always in an effort to notice what is sitting behind it.* (Pause for 30 seconds).

Try to offer your strength and your wisdom to this part of you. Letting this part of you know that there's also this compassionate strength and wisdom now. As best you can—see if you can help this part of you feel supported, validated, and understood and give the reassurance that you're there for it. As the compassionate self, you're not trying to change it or make it go away; you're just holding it compassionately.

Okay, so now just let that hurt part of yourself go—you can thank it for coming and talking. Let's just sit now, mindfully with your compassionate self, focusing on the sense of body slowing down and mind slowing down.

When you are ready, shift your attention back to the room, and open your eyes.

Process in pairs or with the whole group. Ask participants to discuss how this experience went for them, particularly focusing on anything they found difficult (e.g., visualizing the critical part of you, being compassionate toward that part) and any emotions that came up.

When you are ready, shift your attention back to the room, and open your eyes.

Using the Compassionate Self: Experiential Exercise (Using the Compassionate Self)

So, let's come back to these goals of not being lazy, arrogant, and so on (whatever came up as their fears of letting go of self-criticism).

We've established that, although we can occasionally embody these fears, it's not a set of values and goals we would choose. We don't wake up in the morning and think, "Today I really want to be an arrogant, hurtful, and lazy person," right?

Now we're going to do a similar exercise as before when we really got to know our self-critic. But this time, we're going to get in touch with our compassionate self or image—whichever you prefer or seems most helpful.

Now just to remind you, when you move into compassionate self, it really helps to activate the body and brain states if we can. So, first, let's remember to try as best we can to settle into the compassionate self—and create that sense of slowing and grounding in the body. Slow your breath, with an aim to find a comfortable inner rhythm. (Pause.) *Bring to mind your inner wisdom, that we all just find ourselves here with this tricky brain that was not developed by us, and that we are doing the best we can.*

So, we have seen what the critical part of you would like. We also saw that this critic is based mainly in fear or threat. What do you think your compassionate self's wishes for you are?

Process.

Notice the motivation, goals, and values of your compassionate self. Let's imagine our compassionate self or image by once again imagining that you could take this part out of you and see it in front of you. What kind of image forms? What would it look like? What sort of colors arise? What is its presence like? (Pause for about 15–20 seconds.)

Now imagine that it can communicate with you and speak to you. What is it actually saying? What messages does it wish to convey to you? Listen to what your compassionate self/image is saying to you—really let it speak. What does it say? (Pause for about 15–20 seconds.)

As you are listening to this part of you speak with you, what is its voice tone? What sense of emotion do you get from it? Now what does it actually feel for you—what emotions is it directing at you? (Pause for about 15–20 seconds.)

Now how are you feeling about yourself? (Pause for about 15–20 seconds.)

Having a sense of it, hearing it, and noting its feelings for you, what is your sense of what it would like to do with you or for you? (Pause for about 15–20 seconds.)

So now, once again, just being with this image and turning your attention toward this part of you rather than a critical part of you, what are you feeling? In terms of your goals and values, how are you feeling about those? (Pause for about 15–20 seconds.)

And what do you think the chances are of reaching toward your goals or coping when you struggle? (Pause for about 15–20 seconds.)

Process in a similar way to the critical self exercise.

One of the most important things in compassion focused therapy is learning to use mindfulness to notice this unhelpful critical voice and then to switch into compassionate self. Up until now, maybe your critical self and pattern was on autopilot. Learning how to be in touch with your more wise, authoritative, and compassionate pattern—your compassionate mind and your compassionate self will help you deal with things when they don't go according to plan or end in disappointment, as is unfortunately typical of life.

Module 8

Shame and Guilt

REMEMBER: Do not sacrifice the moment for the manual. Be sure to assess and attend to diversity in terms of demographic as well as diagnoses within the group. Be aware of reasons for referral; this will inform fears, blocks, and resistances toward treatment that may arise throughout the duration of the group. This initial awareness of patient presentation and circumstance will allow the group leader(s) to better facilitate cohesion and participation.

Aims:

- Help participants understand that humans have evolved to be social from the first days of life.
- Explore how the threat, drive, and soothing systems are influenced by our social relationships.
- Demonstrate how our threat system is geared for self-monitoring in relation to others. Because of this, we create ideas of what we believe others think of us.
- Explain that shame, guilt, and humiliation are all threat emotions that can arise through our interactions with others. Help participants understand the differences between shame and guilt, and the roots of each.
- Explore how tuning into one's compassionate self can help heal shame and, when appropriate, shift to a reparation-oriented experience of guilt.

Welcome, Grounding, and Personal Practice

Welcome participants to the group.

Short Guidance Soft Landing

> *We are going to begin cultivating compassion with a mindfulness practice. Find a comfortable sitting position and notice how it feels to sit in your chair.* (Short pause.)

DOI: 10.4324/9781003607557-8

Now, we will engage our compassionate body posture.

1. *Sit with a straight back. Keep your head upright and your shoulders in line with your hips. Place your feet flat on the floor.*
2. *Lift your shoulders up and slightly backward.*
3. *Find a comfortable position for your hands that will not be distracting to you.*
4. *Breathe into your belly rather than your chest.*
5. *Bring a friendly facial expression to your body posture.*
6. *Gently fix your gaze on a single spot on the floor or close your eyes if you feel comfortable.*

Now slow and deepen your breath. On each in-breath, say to yourself, with a friendly tone, "Mind slowing down." On each out-breath, say, "Body slowing down." Continue alternating these phrases throughout the practice. Maintain an alert mind even as you try to become stiller, slower, and more grounded.

Allow time for this to settle in. (Longer pause.)

We will now try to develop our inner compassionate mind.

Remember the wisdom that you have been developing in the course so far. We all have tricky brains and certain life experiences that have shaped how our minds and bodies work. Even though our tricky brains and life experiences have affected who we are, we also have minds that can learn how to change and make choices. We are developing the strength and commitment to help ourselves and others deal with the difficulties of life.

Remember why we are in this group: to work on ways to be helpful to ourselves, to support others as best we can on their journey, and to be open to the helpfulness of others. Silently repeat these three flows of compassion back to yourself.

As we bring this practice to a close, connect with your body again. Feel your body in the chair in this moment. Slowly start to come back into the room, and open your eyes when you are ready.

Welcome [back] to Module 8.

Between-Session Practice Check-In

Check that group members were able to engage in between-session practice. Check in to see if any group members thought about or used and part of CFT outside of group. Help the group process their experience, both successes and resistances. You may decide to share a personal reflection on how you integrated ideas from the previous session into your own life.

Process.

Bridge and Forecast

We have now spent time learning how to tune into our compassionate self in order to deal with disappointments and shame-based self-criticism. Now we will explore the nature and function of shame and guilt. We will also discuss how shame can compromise our well-being and ability to learn from mistakes. We will learn how tuning into our compassionate self can aid the process of forgiving ourselves.

Introduction to Shame

Let's do a short practice to focus now on how shame feels. Would anybody be willing to share a personal experience where they felt shame? Try to think of something small that you are okay talking about. (Give time to allow for responses.) *Now everyone imagine what feelings and physical sensations would arise in your body if this experience happened to you.*

What do you imagine other people think about your shameful experience? How do they react? (This is external shame.)

What do you think and feel about yourself? (This is internal shame.)

How do you cope with this situation? (Do you make something up? Lie? Cover things up to avoid shame?)

How has shame influenced your life?

Last time we looked at the issue of self-criticism. We saw that we can constantly monitor ourselves and have negative judgments and feelings toward ourselves. When we learn to be compassionately self-correcting, we can notice things that may not be going well, but we can still encourage and support ourselves to change and improve.

This week we are going to be looking at another set of emotions that can undermine us or damage our relationships, leaving us feeling anxious and depressed rather than inspired to try our best. We call these shame-based emotions. Some aspects of shame-based emotions are linked to self-criticism.

In this module we will be looking at our self-conscious emotions, such as shame and guilt. Before that, let's remember how our minds have evolved and the similarities we have with our animal cousins.

Have you seen any wildlife shows on TV where animals fight with each other over resources? For example, animals often fight over access to the best hunting spots or watering holes. Imagine two lions approaching a watering hole. What happens if one lion feels weaker and more vulnerable than the other? How might it behave in relationship to the stronger lion? What does this behavior look like? Will they be submissive, bold, or afraid?

Process.

Like animals, when we are socially frightened, our bodies go into submissive states. We may want to run away, curl up, or try to hide, especially if we feel under social threat.

However, people don't always go into submissive states like curling up when they experience social threat. Think about what might happen instead of fleeing or submitting. Might someone keep fighting instead of backing down?

Process.

It is clear that we can withdraw or become aggressive when facing social threat. Some people tend to be anxious and submissive, frightened of being criticized. Others are very quick to become aggressive. Interestingly, the more powerful you feel, the more likely you go for power/aggression. For example, bosses are more likely to respond to criticism from subordinates with aggression. On the other hand, if bosses criticize subordinates, the subordinates are more likely to close down, apologize, appease, or even try to hide. Power dynamics are quite important in how we deal with social threats.

Process. Facilitate discussion about these power distinctions. If needed you might give some of the following *optional* examples:

Imagine Maya, a young child, has a mother and father who are quite critical and aggressive toward her. At home she often is blamed when things go wrong. She is quite frightened of her parents. How do you think she will behave when she things they are getting angry with her? How do you think this will affect her later in life?

Process.

Maya may learn to blame herself and try to be submissive in order to protect herself. She will also likely be quite vulnerable to fears of being criticized or rejected. We can also see that Maya might learn to be frightened of her anger because, as a child, her anger could produce a massive counterattack by her parents. It is not her fault that she has learned these behaviors, but it is her responsibility to deal with them.

Process. Check that participants understand this issue of negative self-identity and use the group to explore shame.

Self-Conscious Emotions (Optional)

This optional exercise, provided at the end of the module, introduces the idea of "self-conscious" emotions (e.g., shame).

Internal vs. External Shame

Materials: Handout 8.1
Handout 8.2

> *There are two aspects to shame: internal and external. We may experience external shame if we think that other people look down on us or see us negatively. This is external shame because our shame is related to concerns about our reputation and social standing. In external shame, our attention is on what other people are thinking. It is normal to experience external shame, as all of us have a desire to be valued by others.*

Process. Try to help group members think through the issues of positive and negative social evaluation. In particular, direct them to think about how they may not share their thoughts and feelings for fear of what others will think or how others might respond to them.

> *Because we are constantly concerned about what other people think about us, it might be difficult to be open with our thoughts and emotions. For example, fears about how others see us may stop us from talking or sharing in this group. Have there been any times in group where your fear has stopped you from sharing? What could help you feel comfortable talking openly with the group?*

Process. Help participants talk about how shame is a bodily experience.

> *Now let's think about how external shame affects our bodies. What happens in our bodies if people respond critically and negatively to us? What happens to our heart rate? Where do we look? What happens to our muscles?*
>
> *As we can see, shame is a bodily experience. Our bodies and brains are built to care about what others think of us.*
>
> *Now let's look at how external shame differs from internal shame. In our last module we looked at self-criticism and how we can put ourselves down and feel angry or disappointed in ourselves. We call that internal shame. In other words, our attention is inward, on ourselves and what we are thinking and feeling about ourselves. We can easily remember the critical thoughts and feelings that pop into our heads when we get self-critical (e.g., "You're not as good as you think*

you are!" "You don't try hard enough!" "You're inferior!" "You are lazy!"). It is important for us to understand that underneath all of that self-criticism is actually the fear of external shame, which is the fear of disapproval, social rejection, and isolation.

Process. Check that people understand internal and external shame.

Typically, internal and external shame go together, but not always. For example, we can be very sensitive to external shame without necessarily feeling bad about ourselves. We can also feel bad about ourselves while believing that other people feel good about us.

Give group members 1 minute, then go around the room and write the things people would worry about on the whiteboard. You can then briefly discuss those things and introduce **Handout 8.1**.

Let's now explore this in more detail together. What are you most worried that people think about you? Are you worried about what people might think if they really knew you? Take a minute to think about these questions.

Have patients go to **Handout 8.1**. You may wish to include a personal example of shame from your own life.

We are all social beings that care about what others think of us. Now we are going to do an exercise together to look at this in more detail. Imagine what would happen if I asked you to reveal something here that you felt very ashamed about. I'm not going to actually ask that you reveal this. As you imagine sharing this thing you feel shame about, pay attention to the feelings that arise inside of you. (Pause.)

Now, I'm going to ask you some questions, and I'd like you to put your answers into the table on Handout 8.1. First, what feelings come up for you when you thought you might have to share something shameful?

Process.

How do you think other people would react and treat you if they knew this about you?

Process.

In the moment, how do you react when you feel shame?

Process.

How do you usually cope when you feel shame?

Process.

How has shame influenced your life?

When you finish the exercises, invite group members to fill in each of the boxes (see the following example).

Worked Example from a Group

<table>
<tr><td colspan="3">What feelings come up for me when I thought I might have to share something shameful?

Anxiety, fear, irritation, embarrassment, confusion, discomfort, disgust, etc.</td></tr>
<tr><td>How do I think other people would react and treat me if they knew? (external shame focus)

• She/he is an idiot.
• She/he is disgusting.
• She's/he's not who she/he seems to be.
• She/he is a loser.

Note how we think people will negatively label us

ACTIONS

• People will distance themselves from me.
• People will re-ject me.
• People will certainly not want to get close to me or help me that much.</td><td>In the moment, how do I react when I feel shame? (internal shame focus)

• I'm incompetent.
• I'm inferior.
• I'm not worth knowing.
• I'm careless.
• I'm stupid.
• I'm disgusting.
• I'm unreliable.
• I'm dishonest.

Note how we have these negative labels for ourselves

ACTIONS
• I hide and avoid.
• I try not to think too much about it or ruminate on it.</td><td>How do I usually cope when I feel shame?

• Avoid
• Walk away
• Think of something quite small to share
• Put a positive spin on it
• Hope for the best
• Simply lie</td></tr>
</table>

Notice how shame may not be the only emotion you experience. We can feel a blend of different feelings at once. For example, the fear of revealing our shameful event may be overwhelming and cause us to feel our heart sinking or to freeze up. All of us have this fear around potentially shameful areas of our lives because we are human. There is nothing wrong with us for feeling this, but it can be problematic if we are unable to address it.

Process.

The aim of this exercise is to help participants see that there are multiple emotions associated with shame. It is likely that different people will have different emotions. Some will talk about anxiety and fear, while others might talk about feeling irritated and put on the spot. Others might talk in terms of feeling closed down. Make sure to emphasize that people tend to (1) believe that other people will think negatively about them and (2) distance themselves from people as a result of these fears.

Shame vs. Guilt

Materials: Handout 8.2

We all want to be liked, valued, and accepted. We tend to be triggered into negative emotions if we feel other people are looking down on us, criticizing us, or seeing us negatively. We can also trigger these negative emotions in ourselves with self-criticism. Two common self-conscious emotions we may have in such situations are guilt and shame.

Perhaps one of the most poorly understood self-conscious emotions is guilt. It is often confused with shame; however, shame and guilt are quite different. Guilt is the regret we feel when we have caused harm, and it evolved from the caring system. When mammals evolved caring behavior, they also evolved ways of detecting and avoiding harm to those they cared for. Guilt is a part of this caring system since it inspires us to try to repair any harm that we cause.

With guilt we are not that bothered about whether people like or dislike us. We are not concerned about defending ourselves by submitting, hiding, or fighting. Actually, the emotion of guilt is often accompanied by sadness and remorse, not anxiety or anger. With guilt, we are focused on specific behaviors or harmful things we have done instead of focusing on ourselves as individuals. When we feel guilt, we are focused on repairing the harm that we have done rather on making ourselves feel better.

Note how shame is different from guilt. If we have been harmful and we are trying to repair out of shame, then basically we try to help ourselves feel better. We want the other person to feel better about us, and we want them to forgive us and like us again. We are not really focusing on the harm being caused or the harmed person. Shame tends to be much more self-focused, whereas guilt is behavior-focused. Guilt requires empathy, whereas shame does not. One of the key aspects of shame is that it creates a deep sense of loneliness or disconnection from others.

Process. Help participants understand the difference between shame and guilt by highlighting the following:

- "I am wrong" vs. "I did something wrong"
- Rank or competition mentality vs. care mentality
- Behavioral response: hiding vs. repairing
- Shame = focus on me; guilt = focus on the other

Shame and guilt are not mutually exclusive, and they can blend together. Rarely do single emotions arise. It is far more common that emotions arise as blends.

There is a lot of evidence now that if we can tolerate feeling guilt, then we are able to feel a sense of responsibility and behave morally and in caring and compassionate ways. It is very important that we learn to tolerate guilt without attacking ourselves (i.e., without feeling shame).

Let's look at our fears, blocks, and resistances to guilt. What might they be? Why do we sometimes struggle to tolerate guilt and take responsibility for our mistakes?

Process. Try to guide patients through things that might inhibit their ability to work with guilt. For example, if they really dislike someone, they may not want to feel guilt for having hurt them. Resistance to guilt can be particularly important for those with aggressive/externalizing behaviors.

Imagine that two kids (we'll call them Ty and Isaiah) have both stolen candy from the store and been caught. Ty feels shame because he automatically thinks, "Oh, people will not like me now, and my parents will be angry and not love me!" He is focusing on what others think about him. He might also feel bad about himself (e.g., "I'm a bad person to have done this"). All of his focus is on himself. This is called shame.

Isaiah, on the other hand, does not focus on himself but on the harm that he has done, with a great sense of remorse and sorrow for the pain he has caused. His genuine wish is to try to repair or make amends for his actions. His attention is not on himself but on the harm he has done. This is called guilt.

From this example, we can see that guilt is very important for us because when we allow ourselves to feel to guilt, we are open to recognizing any harm that we have caused other people. This allows us to take responsibility and turn our focus to putting things right, if we can. Remember, in compassion focused therapy, our intention is to try to address suffering. Guilt can help us do this.

Process.

Humiliation (Optional)

This section (at the end of the module) explores what humiliation is.

Example to Further Explore Shame vs. Guilt

We have looked at many different feelings related to external shame, internal shame, and guilt. These can seem a little tricky to understand, so let's think of some examples to help us:

Have participants turn to **Handout 8.2**. The following is an example to help participants understand the difference between shame and guilt. Note: The handout does not differentiate between external and internal shame.

Imagine that you lose your temper with a child and you shout at them. What would a shame response be and what would a guilt response be?

Process. Write answers on board as group members write on handout.

Example: Imagine that you lose your temper with a child and you shout at them.	
Shame Response	**Guilt**
External Shame: Your attention and thinking are focused on the mind of others and on what they are feeling and thinking about you. Your main emotion here is anxiety and embarrassment.	Your attention is on what you did. You are concerned about the feelings of the child. Your focus is on your behavior, not a global sense of self in any way.

Your attention is on what other people who may have witnessed this (e.g., your anger) are thinking and whether they blame you for being a bad person. You might have a sense of being exposed in some way. **Internal Shame:** Your attention is on yourself and possibly blaming yourself for losing control. Your focus is on your qualities rather than just the behavior. Your main emotion here is anxiety or anger, and you feel self-critical. Maybe you notice you that you have a hard time managing your emotions. You may have the thought that you hurt others.	Your emotions are primarily ones of sadness and possibly remorse because this was unintended. (You really didn't want to cause pain to the child.) You are not particularly worried about what others might be thinking about you, and you are not putting yourself down in any way. You see that you can apologize and try to do better next time.

Imagine that you forget your friend's birthday and they call you to remind you. What would a shame response be and what would a guilt response be?

Process. Write answers on board as group members write on handout.

Imagine that because life has become difficult you turn to drugs, and that has negative consequences. What would a shame response be and what would a guilt response be?

Process. Write answers on board as group members write on handout.

How could the compassionate self help you in each of these situations?

Process.

Additional Optional Exercises

Two optional exercises are provided at the end of the module to explore how shame, humiliation, and guilt are different.

Healing Shame

Shifting from Shame to Guilt

Think back to the example you used earlier in which you felt shame. Do not choose anything too large or upsetting, just something you can explore without feeling triggered. Think of this event and try to focus on feelings of sadness and remorse. If the self-critic turns up, just put it to the side.

Sometimes helping people really experience sadness and remorse is very important, as the inability to allow oneself to experience sadness can be a block.

It is important to know that sadness, grief, and remorse are normal processes and that, for many years to come, you will likely feel these emotions about past events. This is normal and even healthy. For example, if we lose someone we love, we do not go to therapy to forget them. Indeed, when they come to mind, we may always have a touch of sadness and regret about losing them. However, over time it becomes more manageable.

Help participants really experience, what at times may be, quite overwhelming sadness and regret. At the same time, help participants focus o not becoming angry or launching attacks on, hating, or being disgusted by the self.

Sharing with the Group (Optional)

This optional exercise, provided at the end of the module, allows patients to share their experiences of shame.

Compassionate Note (Optional)

This optional exercise, provided at the end of the module, involves writing a compassionate note regarding a shameful experience.

Meditation—Reconnecting (Optional)

This optional grounding exercise is provided at the end of the module.

Reviewing Compassion Process

Reminder

You can review the Jordan content from previous modules as needed, or you can go straight to the example from this module. Often a review is not necessary when time is short, and briefly apply the skills learned that day to Jordan's situation is sufficient.

Optional Review

Module 1: Dayroom fight, level drop, anger/anxiety, thinking loops; trick brain, "not my fault but my responsibility"
Module 2: Jordan's red circle scenario (anger); three circles, soothing rhythm-breathing
Module 3: Jordan's rumination on level drop, lingering anger; attention (flashlight), soothing rhythm-breathing
Module 4: Jordan's continuing threat mode; feelings safe through secure place/compassionate other imagery
Module 5: Jordan intentionally shifts to compassion; self-compassion in action (wisdom, strength, commitment)
Module 6: Jordan's dayroom situation produces multiple emotions; compassionate self understands and balances emotions
Module 7: Jordan's self-criticism; understanding inner critic and turning to growth through compassion

Let's see how Jordan deals with shame. After finding out his level had been dropped, Jordan yelled at the staff. He blamed them for keeping him from discharging. After a while, Jordan feels embarrassed about losing his temper. He thinks, "Now the staff will think I'm immature for yelling. They won't like me anymore. What if the other patients heard and now think bad things about me too? That would be so embarrassing." Do you see how self-focused these thoughts are? Here, Jordan is feeling shame. He worries that others are thinking bad things about him. When he is feeling this way, Jordan can use compassion to shift from shame to guilt. With guilt, Jordan thinks, "I shouldn't have yelled at the staff. They are probably doing their best. We all make mistakes, and I should apologize." Guilt helps Jordan want to make amends. Although he still feels bad for losing his temper, he is less focused on what others think and more focused on improving the situation.

Between-Session Practice

Compassionate Intention

As we prepare to develop our compassionate intention:

1. *Sit with a straight back. Keep your head upright and your shoulders in line with your hips. Place your feet flat on the floor.*
2. *Lift your shoulders up and slightly backward.*
3. *Find a comfortable position for your hands that will not be distracting to you.*
4. *Breathe into your belly rather than your chest.*
5. *Bring a friendly facial expression to your body posture.*
6. *Gently fix your gaze on a single spot on the floor or close your eyes if you feel comfortable.*

Now bring your attention to your breathing. Connect with your soothing rhythm-breathing, with your mind slowing down and body slowing down. Pay attention to your mind and body as you do this. Gradually get that sense of grounding with a sense of stilling and slowing but also with an alert mind. Notice yourself becoming more grounded. (Pause.)

Now start connecting with your inner compassionate mind. Remember the wisdom that you have been developing in the course so far. We all have tricky brains and certain life experiences that have shaped how our minds and bodies work. Even though our tricky brains and life experiences have affected who we are, we also have minds that can learn how to change and make choices. We are developing the strength and commitment to help ourselves and others deal with the difficulties of life.

Acknowledge your courage and willingness to embark on this journey of learning, regardless of current circumstances. Acknowledge yourself for being open to learning and growing. You have the courage to stretch your boundaries, even if it's difficult, tricky, and scary. It's scary for everyone. Acknowledge yourself for being here exactly as you are.

You might do this in the form of a wish, something like:

- *May I accept myself in this moment of learning exactly as I am.*
- *May I give myself all the support and all the kindness I need in this moment.*
- *May I accept all of my difficulties and doubts with compassion.*
- *May I give myself all the compassion I need in this moment.*

Remember why we are in this group: to work on ways to be helpful to ourselves, to support others as best we can on their journey, and to be open to the helpfulness of others.

As we bring this practice of developing our compassionate intention to a close, connect with your body again. Feel your body in the chair in this moment. Slowly start to come back into the room, and open your eyes when you are ready.

Pause

How was that? When might this exercise be helpful to you? (Give a moment for responses.)

Process.

Optional Materials

Introduction to Shame: Self-Conscious Emotions

Now that we know that some of what we experience when we feel under certain types of social threats are a result of the way our brains are built, we can begin to explore different aspects of how we experience social threats.

These are called self-conscious or social emotions, and they are linked to our feelings about ourselves. For example, we might be frightened of slipping on the ice or being bitten by a snake. These are basic or primary fears. However, if we are frightened of being rejected because people don't like us, then this is called a self-conscious emotion. There is typically no physical danger associated with the self-conscious emotion.

Self-conscious emotions can be positive as well as negative. For example, on the positive side, pride is linked to the feeling that other people admire or like you in some way. The family of shame-related emotions are on the negative side and are connected to things we feel about ourselves if we think other people do not approve of us.

Typically, when we feel shame, we feel it in a global sense of ourselves rather than just being a bit disappointed in how we have behaved. For example, if we feel ashamed about our appearance for some reason, we don't think, "I'm not as attractive as I want to be." We typically think we are ugly or unattractive. In shame we have a sense of becoming something quite negative.

Internal vs. External Shame

External Shame:

- Our attention is on what other people are thinking
- It is normal, all of us care about how others view us
- Fear of disapproval, social rejection, and isolation
- Makes it difficult to be open with our thoughts and emotions

Shame is a bodily experience. What happens in your body when you feel shame?

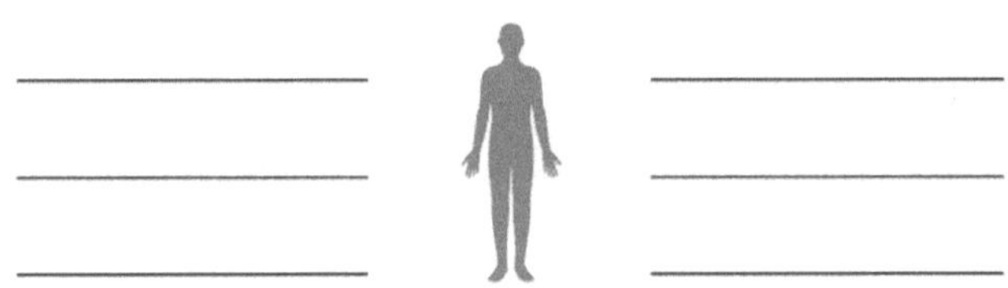

Internal Shame:

- Our attention is inwards, on ourselves
- Self-criticism
- Underneath is the fear of external shame

Handout 8.1 Internal vs. External Shame

Exploring Shame

What feelings come up for me when I thought I might have to share something shameful?

How do I think other people would react and treat me if they knew?	In the moment, how do I react when I feel shame?	How do I usually cope when I feel shame?

How has shame influenced my life?

Handout 8.2 Exploring Shame

Shame vs. Guilt

For the situations below, write a shame- and guilt-based responses to each. Think about which you would be most helpful.

Imagine that you lose your temper with a child, and you shout at them.

Shame response: ______________________________

Guilt response: ______________________________

Imagine that you forget your friend's birthday, and they call you up to remind you.

Shame response: ______________________________

Guilt response: ______________________________

Imagine that because life has become difficult you turn to drugs, and that has negative consequences.

Shame response: ______________________________

Guilt response: ______________________________

Think of how your compassionate-self could help you in each situation.

Handout 8.3 Shame vs. Guilt

Shame vs. Guilt: Humiliation

There is another set of emotions that we can experience when people criticize us or treat us rudely or badly—when we feel others are shaming us. What do you think that might be?

Process. Encourage participants to generate the externalizing of hostile emotions.

Suppose someone put you down unfairly. What emotion might arise in you?

Process. Help participants to focus on the anger of external shame.

What happens to our attention when we feel anger toward other people who we might think are externally shaming or disapproving of us?

Process.

We call this humiliation, which is linked to shame, but different. When we experience humiliation and the anger associated with humiliation, our attention is on the mind of the other person, as it is with external shame. However, with humiliation we feel the desire to attack instead of wanting to appease or submit. We might have thoughts of "How dare they!" "What gives them the right to do this!" "They are unreasonable!" or "I'm going to get back at them!" In other words, just as we may want to flee, hide, run away, or avoid people in response to certain shame situations; we may also have the urge to fight or attack.

Process.

Let's think together about situations that we might find humiliating and that might stimulate anger in us.

Process. Help participants think of situations where they felt a sense of humiliation.

At this point, we are not wanting to enter into complex emotional memories but to just touch on these feelings.

If someone has treated us unfairly, what might stop us from expressing our anger?

Process. Discuss how group members may be ashamed of their anger because they may be frightened of what other people will think or do if they express it. You can invite them to have discussions around early life on these themes.

Shame vs. Guilt: Additional Optional Exercises

Optional Exercise #1: You can also use the Christmas shoppers example here.

- If the shop assistant is very rude to you, you may have any of the following reactions:
  - External shame: feeling that you have done something wrong to upset them
  - Internal shame: blaming yourself because you are not assertive enough
  - Humiliation: feeling anger at them and threatening them back
  - Guilt: feeling sadness that you have done something that has caused them pain in some way

Process. Help participants think through why all of these could arise but some would be unhelpful and why. Help them think through how assertiveness, which will come in a module later, is not the same as responding to humiliation.

Optional Exercise #2: You can give scenarios and ask participants:

- What would a shame response be like?
- What would a guilt response be like?
- What would a humiliation response be like?
- Which of those do you think your emotions would be if you really allowed yourself to feel genuinely sorry and remorseful for your behavior?

Process. Try to think of other examples and invite group members to discuss what would be going through their mind if they were focused on external shame, internal shame, guilt, or humiliation.

Healing Shame: Sharing with the Group

Give instructions to have all participants activate the compassionate self. From the position of the compassionate self, ask everyone (including group leaders) to share a real shame experience or something they are ashamed of in group (nothing too triggering of course). Make sure there is an atmosphere of compassionate understanding—if necessary, by repeating the compassionate self-induction. Valiate each sharing.

Process.

Healing Shame: Compassionate Note

Have group members write a compassionate note to themselves regarding a shameful experience.

Process.

Healing Shame: Meditation—Reconnecting

Start by closing your eyes and feeling how you sit in your chair right now.

Settle into your compassion posture with your back straight, shoulders in line with your hips, and an open chest. Now start slowing your breath, and with each slower and deeper breath, say, with a friendly tone, "Mind slowing down" and then "Body slowing down." Alternate these phrases on each out-breath. Gradually feel a sense of stilling/slowing, but also a mental alertness. Notice yourself becoming more grounded and stable—as stable as a mountain.

Let your awareness expand to include your whole body. Try to feel or sense the whole of yourself—of your presence. Turn your attention to each part of the body, moving your awareness through the sensations of your head and torso, your arms and hands, and your legs and feet.

Again, try to combine the awareness you feel in each part of your body into a cohesive sense of the whole of yourself—the existential experience of "I am." Feel your body sitting here in this room. Stay with this experience for several breaths.

Now let awareness expand to include your environment. First, feel the air around you. For several breaths feel the air as it touches your body.

Notice how the same air touches everybody in the room and connects you with the group. Sense the presence of the people around you for several breaths.

Now, bring to mind the wisdom that we are all human beings. Like all the millions and billions of human beings outside this room, we all have experiences of shame, discomfort, anger, and anxiety. We all have experiences we would not want to share with others. Shame is a shared life challenge that we can all struggle with and face. We all have vulnerabilities, weaknesses, and flaws. We all make mistakes. We all sometimes struggle with aspects of our personality. We are all part of this flow of life. At the same time, we are here, together, facing this deeply isolating emotion with the strength, wisdom, and commitment of the compassionate self. Just being here, as we are, is a sign that we are starting to approach this emotion with the willingness to heal.

Experience the connectedness with the group and all other human beings for several breaths.

Now start tuning in to your inner compassionate mind. Bring to mind, attend to, and remember the wisdom that you have been developing in the course so far: that we all just find ourselves here with a very tricky brain and certain life experiences that have shaped how our minds and bodies work—shaping the version of ourselves that we are. However, we also have a mind that can learn how to change and make choices, so we are developing the strength and commitment to help ourselves and others address and deal with life and inner difficulties.

Process.

Module 9

Deepening Compassion for the Self

REMEMBER: **Do not sacrifice the moment for the manual.** Be sure to assess and attend to diversity in terms of demographic as well as diagnoses within the group. Be aware of reasons for referral; this will inform fears, blocks, and resistances toward treatment that may arise throughout the duration of the group. This initial awareness of patient presentation and circumstance will allow the group leader(s) to better facilitate cohesion and participation.

Aims:

- Deepen self-compassion.
- Practice strategies to more readily access and generalize self-compassion.

Welcome, Grounding, and Personal Practice

Welcome participants to the group.

Short Guidance Soft Landing

Let's take a moment to revisit our intention to develop our compassionate mind. We start by closing our eyes. We feel how we sit in our chair right now. (Pause for 15 seconds.)

Settle into your compassion posture. Sit with your back straight and shoulders in line with your hips. Now slow your breathing. With each slower and deeper breath say, slowly and with a friendly tone, "Mind slowing down" and then "Body slowing down." Alternate these phrases on each out-breath. Notice a sense of grounding, stilling, and slowing. Remember to keep an alert mind. Notice yourself becoming more grounded. (Pause.)

DOI: 10.4324/9781003607557-9

Start tuning into your inner compassionate self. Bring to mind the wisdom that you have been developing in the course so far. We all find ourselves here with a very tricky brain. We all have had certain life experiences that have shaped how our minds and bodies work. But we can learn how to change and make different choices. So, we are developing strength, authority, and commitment. We use these qualities to help ourselves and others to deal with life and inner difficulties.

So, as we are sitting here, we also say in a friendly and committed way:

I am coming here today and over the next weeks in order to:

- *Develop compassion for myself.* (Pause.)
- *Increase compassion for others.* (Pause.)
- *Be open to compassion from others.* (Pause.)

Okay, now start to let these thoughts and motivations go. Start to come back slowly into the room. Notice your body in the chair and feet on the ground. When you are ready, you can open your eyes.

Between-Session Practice Check-In

Check that group members were able to engage in between-session practice. Check in to see if any group members thought about or used and part of CFT outside of group. Help the group process their experience, both successes and resistances. You may decide to share a personal reflection on how you integrated ideas from the previous session into your own life.

Welcome [back] to Module 9.

Bridge and Forecast

If beneficial, you can briefly walk through key take aways from all previous modules, to look at how all the things that have been learned to this point connect together.

We have explored the nature and the function of shame and guilt. We've also discussed how shame can compromise our well-being and ability to learn from mistakes. We will now learn how to tune into ourselves from the perspective of our compassionate self. We'll write a letter to ourselves from our compassionate self and learn how to strengthen our abilities to approach ourselves compassionately.

Exploring Self-Compassion

The goal of this section is to help participants purposefully shift mental states using their bodies (e.g., posture and breathing). Help them explore why and how developing self-compassion is helpful.

Today we're going to be looking more deeply and working more closely with developing compassion for ourselves. In general, what has your experience been with using self-compassion?

Process.

Can we briefly revisit the reasons that we are coming here and practicing compassion?

Process. Link back to what group members discussed in the first session, including hopes for the group.

Like we've been talking about before, we are all humans who are made by our genes that we didn't choose. We didn't choose the bodies we were born into. We didn't choose to be born into this culture at this time. We didn't choose to have our brain with the emotions that it's capable of.

This means that the first step in self-compassion, then, is to remember that it's not our fault, but it's our responsibility. The genes we were born with and the situations we were born into have shaped us, perhaps in ways that we do not like. That is not our fault. As we recognize how we are shaped by genes and situations that we cannot control, we can have greater compassion for ourselves. We can be kinder to ourselves as we realize that we are not at fault for the things that have shaped us into who we are.

Process.

The second step in self-compassion is to recognize that we all have a motivation for caring and compassion. This compassion can help us remember that it's not our fault that tricky and threat-based stuff gets activated in our minds. As we learn to apply this motivation for caring to ourselves, we can be more self-compassionate. Remember our definition of compassion—it is that we are sensitive to the suffering of self and others and that we make a commitment to try the best we can to alleviate and prevent such suffering. At its simplest, compassion is the desire to be helpful, not harmful, to self and others. Some of us find it easier to be compassionate toward others but forget to be compassionate toward ourselves.

For a minute, think about the extent over the last few weeks that you have noticed yourself trying to be helpful rather than harmful. Don't worry if you feel it hasn't gone so well; that's just how it is. Try to bring to mind times over the past few weeks when you were helpful even in small ways. This could be to friends, family, children, or even strangers.

Just try for a moment to switch into that part of yourself that would like to be helpful. How does this feel?

Process.

Okay, so now let's take that same idea of compassion and try to apply it to ourselves. Sometimes, it can be hard to have compassion for ourselves, like when we have a habit of being critical and blaming ourselves. People who have experienced trauma often have difficulty with compassion toward themselves. Let's really try to tap into the version of ourselves that can be self-compassionate and respect our unique situation. What is this like?

Process. Remember to explore blocks and resistances, identifying them as such for participants. Support participants in brainstorming ways to address these resistances when they arise.

Take a minute and look back over the past few weeks and try to bring to mind times when you've tried to be helpful and understanding toward yourself rather than being neglectful, hurtful, or harmful. You may think about times that you practiced your breathing, times you thought kindly about yourself and your situation, times you were more careful with your self-criticism, etc. How do you feel as you think about this?

Deepening Compassionate Exercises

Materials: Handout 9.1
Handout 9.2

Compassionate Letter-Writing

Note for the Group Leader

The Compassionate Letter-Writing exercise is typically completed in this module. However, use clinical judgment in deciding if this exercise is appropriate for your group's writing level. If you do not think that this exercise is appropriate, use Compassion at the Mirror as an alternative exercise.

If group leaders prefer, the Compassionate Letter-Writing exercise can be finished between-sessions for practice. The success of this intervention depends on the participants' ability to access their compassionate self. At this point, it would be good to assess the group's ability to move out of the threat system into the soothing system. It would also be helpful for them to be able to have a solid understanding and ability to access the compassionate self through imagery. If those capabilities are not intact, it might be better to do this intervention after practicing the soothing rhythm-breathing and imagery exercises from earlier modules (e.g., from Modules 2, 4, and 5).

Today, we have been able to go into our compassionate mind and generate helpful coping ideas for when we're struggling. Try to remember that we can access the compassionate mind through our breathing, grounding, and wisdom.

Ask participants to open up to **Handout 9.1**. Make sure to have pens available.

This letter-writing activity is written as an exercise for pairs. It can alternatively be done as an individual exercise where group members simply write a letter and then move into the compassionate self. If you chose to do this, adjust the following wording accordingly. Once in compassionate self, have the group members read the letter to themselves very slowly and deliberately.

Now we're going to write a letter to ourselves from our compassionate self. Letter-writing can be really helpful because when we write, we use different parts of our mind and brain. Sometimes when we write to ourselves, we can see things in new ways, or we may have new insights occur to us.

To prepare us for this exercise, let's access our compassionate mind. Try to feel that part of you that can be kind and understanding of others. Try to see how you would be and act if you were caring for someone you like. Consider your general manner, facial expressions, voice tone, and feelings that come with your caring self. Spend a few moments really thinking about this and trying to feel in contact with this part of yourself. (Pause.)

Check for agreement to this. If patients do not want to work in pairs, you can make the exercise individual. Group leaders may rotate working with each individual group member to help each walk through the process.

This exercise has a number of parts to it. We will be writing a supportive letter to ourselves about a life difficulty. We will be reading these letters in pairs. Once you have written your letter, we will stop, ensure that we are in our compassionate-self state again, and read the letter that you wrote out loud to your partner. Once you've read your letter to them, they will then read their letter to you. Finally, you will exchange letters so that each of you will read your partner's letter to them and your partner will read your letter to you.

Think of something that you want support or understanding with—something that makes you feel shame, self-critical, or not good enough. This is a supportive letter, directing compassion toward yourself in dealing with this difficulty.

Pause and ensure that all group members have selected something to write about, providing guidance or cues (e.g., "Maybe something happened in the last couple days that was tough to deal with or put you into the red circle. You could write about that").

You might notice that starting this letter can be a little tricky, so just start writing anything you want. You can start by writing your name: "Dear ________," and you can write in any way you want. There is no right or wrong way to do this, though here are a few pointers. (Write the following on the board.)

1. *Avoid giving yourself advice or saying what you "should," "need to," or "must" do.*
2. *Focus on your courage and your strengths.*
3. *Notice opportunities to be helpful to yourself.*

> *Some of you might worry about your spelling, grammar, or other potential issues with the letter. These things don't matter for this exercise.*
> *Does all that make sense?*

Once people seem clear about what they're trying to do, and you've clarified the point and structure of the letter, given them five to seven minutes to write (or however long is needed).

At the end of the writing time, invite group members to take a moment of silence to reactivate the compassionate self again.

Invite Person A to read their letter to Person B and given them a couple of minutes to process. At the end of that, invite Person B to read their letter to Person A. Again, give a couple of minutes to process.

> *Here are some pens and paper.* (Pause.) *As you start writing, you may be aware of all kinds of distractions that will pull you off course, such as being critical, feeling you won't do it right, or feeling that you are being silly. Whatever distraction or resistance comes up, try to remember that all of those thoughts can steer your mind away from the task of being compassionate. When you notice your mind being distracted or critical, just try to pull it back to the task at hand as best you can. It's okay that your mind does this.*

At the end of that, have each person read the letter that their partner wrote with the compassionate intent we've discussed earlier. Give a few minutes for processing.

> *When you are reading your letter back to the person you are paired with, try as best you can to read it in the mindset of the compassionate self. So, you will be reading it slower than you normally would, with a deeper breathing pattern, and with a genuine desire to be helpful. You'll read it with the compassionate wish that you will create the kindest feeling that you possibly can as you say the words.*
>
> *Now, as you read the letter of the person you are paired with back to them, read it back to them as compassionately as you can. This means you will be reading it slower than you would normally, with a genuine compassion intention. Try to do this with a kind voice tone. Really tune into the issues that the person has been writing about if you can.*
>
> *When you are listening and hearing your own letter coming back to you, try to stay with your compassionate mindset, really listening to the importance of what you've* written. (Allow time for reading.)

So, let's explore this in stages. What was it like writing the letter from your compassionate mind?

What was it like getting into your compassionate mind again and really paying attention to what you'd written and noticing the wisdom in what you had written to yourself?

What was it like hearing somebody else read your letter back?

Process.

Compassionate Flash Cards

We've seen that we can take a life difficulty, shift into our compassionate mind states, and try to generate some ideas that would be helpful to us. We are also able to think about those helpful ideas from a compassionate-self mindset. While doing this, we can continue to remind ourselves that life can be very difficult without any easy answers, but we are trying to do the best we can.

We're going to try another exercise to increase self-compassion. Bring to mind a life difficulty. Again, nothing too major—the idea is always to challenge yourself but not to overwhelm yourself. From the position of your compassionate mind, how would you ideally like to deal with this difficulty? We recognize that we often can't make things go away like anxiety or other uncomfortable experiences, but we can learn to tolerate and cope with them in different ways that are more helpful. (Pause.)

Without blaming or shaming but just focusing on trying to be helpful, how understanding are you of this difficulty? Could you be more understanding, more empathic toward yourself? What would that be like? (Pause.)

Now let's use our empathy and understanding. What do you need to know and what would be helpful to you right now to deal with this difficulty? (Pause.)

Invite group to share and collaboratively discuss helpful responses to these difficulties. Write the responses on the board.

So, now we are going to think about applying these ideas, building compassionate behavior into our everyday living. As a group, let's generate some ideas about how we could practice certain behaviors during the week that would be examples of compassionate behavior. Let's remind ourselves that when we think and react from a compassionate mindset, even when we don't necessarily feel like doing so. Our behaviors can shift as well.

Write the responses on the board. Compassionate behaviors can look like carrying behaviors that one would typically do for a relative. Inquire what would make a behavior compassionate (according to the definition and understanding of compassion acquired thus far). Ask participants to open up to **Handout 9.2** to write down compassionate ideas/strategies onto flash cards.

> *Let's turn these compassionate ideas and strategies into a flash card. To do this, we're going to think of three or four really helpful statements, ideas, or actions that would be useful for you to remember and to say in a compassionate way at the time you need them. Consider a difficulty that is ongoing, or something you anticipate might put you into red circle. What would you like to do or remind yourself of when this happens? Maybe you want to draw on some of the ideas we came up with as a group. It's okay to borrow from other compassionate people and other situations. If you're unsure, you can ask others in the group for their ideas too.*

Process. Help participants see how this is different from coping skills that they may have learned in the past. The compassionate self provides a new state of mind.

> *Now that you have generated some helpful statements, ideas, and actions, let's move into the compassionate mindset and really focus on thinking through those ideas. Try saying some of these with a compassionate intention with a kind and gentle voice tone that has a deep wisdom and understanding.*
>
> *Write these things down in Handout 9.2. For some, it might be useful to pull out this page and hang it up in your room where you can see these compassionate ideas and strategies every day.*

Compassionate Breathing and Compassionate Color (Optional)

This optional exercise, provided at the end of the module, uses breathing and imagery of a compassionate light, energy, or mist to increase self-compassion.

Compassion at the Mirror (Optional)

This optional exercise, provided at the end of the module, involves using a mirror to increase self-compassion.

Reviewing Compassion Process

Reminder

You can review the Jordan content from previous modules as needed, or you can go straight to the example from this module. Often a review is not necessary when time is short, and briefly apply the skills learned that day to Jordan's situation is sufficient.

Optional Review

Module 1: Dayroom fight, level drop, anger/anxiety, thinking loops; trick brain, "not my fault but my responsibility"
Module 2: Jordan's red circle scenario (anger); three circles, soothing rhythm-breathing
Module 3: Jordan's rumination on level drop, lingering anger; attention (flashlight), soothing rhythm-breathing
Module 4: Jordan's continuing threat mode; feelings safe through secure place/compassionate other imagery
Module 5: Jordan intentionally shifts to compassion; self-compassion in action (wisdom, strength, commitment)
Module 6: Jordan's dayroom situation produces multiple emotions; compassionate self understands and balances emotions
Module 7: Jordan's self-criticism; understanding inner critic and turning to growth through compassion
Module 8: Jordan's shame from yelling at the staff; compassion to switch to guilt and remedy situation

Now let's think of how to apply what we have been learning today to Jordan's situation. As Jordan feels upset, he remembers that there are many ways to increase self-compassion. One method he tries is compassionate letter-writing. He writes about how difficult it has been having his level dropped. In his letter, he expresses compassion toward himself. He acknowledges his anger. He tells himself that it is normal to feel angry. Then he reassures himself that everything will be okay. Jordan reads his letter when he feels angry about his level. It helps him feel compassion and love. It makes him feel understood. Jordan is taking responsibility for his well-being as he uses these skills.

Between-Session Practice

Generating Compassion

As we prepare to develop our compassionate intention:

1. *Sit with a straight back. Keep your head upright and your shoulders in line with your hips. Place your feet flat on the floor.*
2. *Lift your shoulders up and slightly backward.*
3. *Find a comfortable position for your hands that will not be distracting to you.*
4. *Breathe into your belly rather than your chest.*
5. *Bring a friendly facial expression to your body posture.*
6. *Gently fix your gaze on a single spot on the floor or close your eyes if you feel comfortable.*

Now bring your attention to your breathing. Connect with your soothing rhythm-breathing, with your mind slowing down and body slowing down. Pay attention to your mind and body as you do this. Gradually get that sense of grounding with a sense of stilling and slowing, but also with an alert mind. Notice yourself becoming more grounded. (Longer pause.)

Now start connecting with your inner compassionate mind. Remember the wisdom that you have been developing in the course so far. We all have tricky brains and certain life experiences that have shaped how our minds and bodies work. Even though our tricky brains and life experiences have affected who we are, we also have minds that can learn how to change and make choices. We are developing the strength and commitment to help ourselves and others deal with the difficulties of life.

Acknowledge your courage and willingness to embark on this journey of learning, regardless of current circumstances. Acknowledge yourself for being open to learning and growing. You have the courage to stretch your boundaries, even if it's difficult, tricky, and scary. It's scary for everyone. Acknowledge yourself for being here exactly as you are.

You might do this in the form of a wish, something like:

- *May I accept myself in this moment of learning exactly as I am.*
- *May I give myself all the support and all the kindness I need in this moment.*

- *May I accept all of my difficulties and doubts with compassion.*
- *May I give myself all the compassion I need in this moment.*

Gently ask yourself, "[Name], what do you want to take home from today's session?" Think about what lessons from this session will be the most helpful to you. Listen to whatever arises with curiosity.

Remember why we are in this group: to work on ways to be helpful to ourselves, to support others as best we can on their journey, and to be open to the helpfulness of others. Silently repeat these three flows of compassion back to yourself.

As we bring this practice of developing our compassionate intention to a close, connect with your body again. Feel your body in the chair in this moment. Slowly start to come back into the room, and open your eyes when you are ready. (Pause.)

When might an exercise like this be helpful?

Process.

Optional Material

Deepening Compassion Exercises: Compassionate Breathing and Compassionate Color

We are now going to explore a practice for deepening our self-compassion.

Remember, as with all our practices, we want to do this mindfully. This means that when our minds wander somewhere else, which they will do, that we simply notice the wandering and we gently and compassionately bring them back on task. No need to stress about our wandering minds. We just want to focus and observe as best we can. If your mind is highly distracted with worries or feelings, try to just bring your mind back and acknowledge that sometimes these aspects of our mind have very strong pulls.

So, sit in your chair with your compassionate posture of shoulders back, open diaphragm, and concave curve in the back, and allow your breath to come down deeper into your diaphragm. Find your soothing rhythm-breathing rate at around five breaths per minute, even and regular. (Pause maybe for a minute or so.)

Now just focus on the fact that the breath coming into you is also life-sustaining. Without it, you would die, of course. Stay with the idea

Compassionate Letter

1. **Think** about something that makes you feel shame, self-critical, or not good enough.
2. **Notice** how it makes you feel.
3. **Activate** your compassionate-self.
4. **Write** a compassionate letter to yourself.

Dear ___________,

From ___________

Handout 9.1 Compassionate Letter-Writing

Compassionate Flashcards

Write down three or four really helpful statements, ideas, or actions that would help you feel compassion during a difficult time.

Handout 9.2 Compassionate Flash Cards

that you are breathing in a way that sustains you. Imagine you are taking in life-giving breath and try to feel that breath really sustaining you. With each breath you are taking in air that will really help you. Feel its life-giving properties move around in your lungs and maybe even flowing around your body to sustain you and to support you. (Pause maybe for a minute or so.)

Now imagine that you are surrounded by a compassionate light, mist, or energy. As you breathe in, you are breathing in this compassionate light, mist, or energy and allowing it to move around in your body, bringing compassion to all parts of your body. We have compassion in our lungs, compassion in our heart, compassion in our stomach, compassion down into the legs. And imagine that as you breathe in the compassionate light, mist, or energy that it is also going up into your head filling your head with its compassionate soothing energy. (Pause maybe for a minute or so.)

Now imagine that this compassionate light, mist, or energy is soothing, but also trying to heal. That is its job and function. Just like water can wash away things in its path, imagine that healing is the function of this light, mist, or energy. It has no other motivation than to heal you, soothe you, and help all the parts of your body including your mind that may be suffering in various ways. (Pause maybe for a minute or so.)

Now imagine your whole body is made of this compassionate light, mist, or energy and you have a body of light. It might be a bright light, or it may have a color—whatever seems good for you. (Pause maybe for a minute or so.)

Process.

Sometimes when we think of our compassionate self, it can be helpful to think or our self with this compassionate energy or light in it. When we begin to deepen the compassionate self, we are deepening our sense of being connected to the world around us; even the air we breathe is fundamental to our existence. We are a part of the flow of life.

Deepening Compassion Exercises: Compassion at the Mirror

Note for the Group Leader

Research suggests that looking at ourselves from an external point of view can facilitate the emergence of compassion toward ourselves.

In this exercise, we will try to look at our own reflection from the perspective of our compassionate self, constantly shifting from an "analytic" perspective to a compassionate perspective.

We tend to look at ourselves in the mirror only in an analytical way, trying to spot imperfections or to observe details. Not very often (or maybe ever) do we look at our own face in its fullness, like we usually observe other people's faces, from an external point of view.

The way we view other people and the way others view us are generally more friendly and compassionate than the way we normally look at ourselves. In a sense, our own view of ourselves can be biased by many experiences, memories, and conditioning that make the perception of ourselves almost distorted.

Process. For an example, look at this video: https://www.youtube.com/watch?v=litXW91UauE

We will now use a mirror to really "meet" ourselves and to facilitate that empathetic process. Keep in mind that it is very likely that many resistances will arise, and we may notice a desire to fix things we don't like (blue system). We might have painful feelings about the things on our face that we don't like (red system). Remember that such responses are completely natural; actually, they are at the core of this practice. Our practice of becoming more compassionate toward ourselves becomes stronger every time we commit to meet with compassion the many resistances to the practice itself.

Our goal is to constantly come back, over and over to our compassionate mind: how would our compassionate-self look at our self, especially in a moment of suffering? What kind of gaze would she/he have on us? Or how would we look at the face of a friend in a moment of suffering? Would we look at imperfections in her or his face? So, the practice helps us move toward compassionate intention to the suffering and the painful emotions that our face might express.

Take your mirror and, at first, just look at yourself in the way you would normally. Where does your attention go? What are the thoughts that pop up into your mind? Are they critical thoughts?

Now close your eyes and settle into your compassion posture with your back straight and shoulders in line with your hips while opening your diaphragm. Now slow your breathing, and with each slower and deeper breath say, slowly and with a friendly tone, "Mind slowing down" and then "Body slowing down."

Now bring to mind, attend to, and remember the wisdom that you have been developing in the course so far: that we all just find ourselves here with a very tricky brain and certain life experiences that have shaped how our minds and bodies work. Refocus on the desire to help, to alleviate the suffering that you encounter as best as you can. Refocus on the strength and commitment to help ourselves and others address and deal with life and inner difficulties.

Now, from this position of inner wisdom and strength, and with the only intention to give support, to help and to try to alleviate the suffering that you meet, gently open your eyes. Commit to look at your own face in the mirror from the perspective of your compassionate self.

What does your compassionate self notice of that face in the mirror? (Pause for 15 seconds.)

Does your compassionate self notice any sign of discomfort or suffering? (Pause for 15 seconds.)

The compassionate self is really interested and able to see what is behind those eyes. What does she/he see? What are the needs that those eyes express? (Pause for 15 seconds.)

Now, really connecting with the deep desire to bring relief, to say something that could really help that person in the mirror, and connecting with the warm wisdom and the strength, what kind of facial expression would your compassionate self have toward that suffering person? (Pause for 15 seconds.)

What kind of smile? (Pause for 15 seconds.)

What kind of gaze could express all the deep understanding and the desire to help your compassionate self has? (Pause for 15 seconds.)

Now, if the compassionate self had to say something to that person in the mirror, something that comes from the heartfelt desire to be of support and of help, and to bring some kind of relief to that suffering person, what would she/he say? What would be the words that person would really need to hear in this very moment? Whisper it, as best as you can, with the intention to bring help, support, relief, or maybe courage. (Pause for 15 seconds.)

Use the compassionate intention as an anchor: every time your mind wanders away, simply realize that it's normal. Kindly come back to the commitment to meet that face and those eyes in the mirror with a compassionate intention. Indeed, you probably would not stop trying to convey your intent to care for a friend, even if at the beginning she/he felt reluctant. Actually, the core of this exercise is to kindly and patiently work with that reluctance, and to stick with our compassionate intent toward our suffering, especially when we feel embarrassment or we think we don't deserve it.

If you feel that the practice is becoming too intense, just close your eyes again and connect to your soothing rhythm-breathing. Gently remember that it's natural to feel resistances, that it is not your fault: our brains and our experiences have often made us reluctant and even afraid to experience certain types of emotion. Just welcome this resistance and come back to the intention to meet with compassion the suffering that you might notice in your own eyes. And when you are ready, you can open up your eyes again and tell yourself again the compassionate phrases that you have used before, or some other phrases that you might feel more appropriate now.

Gentle repetition is important to really convey a sense of "I'm really here for you," especially when resistances arise.

Process.

Module 10

Compassionate Assertiveness

REMEMBER: **Do not sacrifice the moment for the manual.** Be sure to assess and attend to diversity in terms of demographic as well as diagnoses within the group. Be aware of reasons for referral; this will inform fears, blocks, and resistances toward treatment that may arise throughout the duration of the group. This initial awareness of patient presentation and circumstance will allow the group leader(s) to better facilitate cohesion and participation.

Aims:

Introduce group members to the concept of compassionate assertiveness. In this module, we examine:

- What assertiveness is and what it is not
- How assertiveness ties into the strength and authority of compassion
- Fears and resistances of assertiveness
- How to use helpful communication patterns (rather than passive/submissive or aggressive patterns)
- How we can say no with assertive communication

Welcome, Soft Landing, and Personal Practice

Welcome participants to the group.

Short Guidance Soft Landing

As usual, we will begin with a soft landing. Let's be aware of the experience and intentionally develop our compassionate mind.

Go ahead and get comfortable in your chairs, feet flat on the floor, sitting straight, shoulders back, and chest open. If you are comfortable, gently close your eyes, or if you prefer, just direct your gaze downward.

DOI: 10.4324/9781003607557-10

Now just start to slow down your breathing. Next, start to settle your mind and body.

Remember your compassionate body posture, facial expression, and voice tone.

Now, let's move into our soothing rhythm-breathing. I will count you into this by saying: "In, 2, 3; out, 2, 3. In, 2, 3, 4; out 2, 3, 4. In, 2, 3, 4, 5; out, 2, 3, 4, 5." (Count about 1 second apart—remember to keep your counting steady.)

As you develop your comfortable rhythm, notice and focus on the feeling of inner slowing with each out-breath. Gradually get that sense of grounding—a sense of stilling and slowing with an alert mind. Notice yourself becoming more grounded.

Say, in your mind, on each alternate out-breath in a friendly and supportive voice: "Body slowing down . . . Mind slowing down."

Tune into your inner compassion—attend to and remember the wisdom that you have been developing in the group so far. We all just find ourselves here with a very tricky brain and certain life experiences that have shaped how our minds and bodies work. We can learn how to change and make choices—we can develop the strength, authority, and commitment to help ourselves and others deal with life and inner difficulties.

And now, just connect with that deep compassionate motivation and say to yourself in a friendly and committed way:

I am coming here today and over the next weeks in order to:

- *Develop compassion for myself.* (Pause.)
- *Increase compassion for others.* (Pause.)
- *Be open to compassion from others.* (Pause.)

Now, I invite you to think of someone you care about. Bring this person to your mind as if they were standing here, right in front of you.

While keeping this person in mind, try to send this person the following compassionate wishes from all your heart:

- *May you be happy.*
- *May you be free of suffering.*
- *May you be healthy and strong.*
- *May you be able to live in this world peacefully, joyfully, with ease.*

Between-Session Practice Check-In

Check that group members were able to engage in between-session practice. Check in to see if any group members thought about or used and part of CFT outside of group. Help the group process their experience, both successes and resistances. You may decide to share a personal reflection on how you integrated ideas from the previous session into your own life.

Okay, now start to let this exercise go. Start coming back slowly into the room, noticing your body in the chair, feet on the ground, and when you are ready, you can open your eyes.

Welcome [back] to Module 10.

Bridge and Forecast

So far, we have been spending time in group strengthening our compassionate self. Our compassionate self can help us to feel grounded and can also help to balance our multiple emotions. Today, we're going to build on these skills by focusing on compassionate assertiveness. Some people might think that to be compassionate, you have to always be nice and do what other people say. Some may also think that to be compassionate, they don't really say what their needs are. This is actually not what compassion is at all.

In fact, compassion is not weak. Often, when people hear the word assertive, they may think of someone being rude or aggressive. Compassionate assertiveness is not aggression, nor is it about "giving in" or being submissive. Compassionate assertiveness is learning to be clear about your values, wishes, wants, and needs. Compassionate assertiveness is being able to ask for these things or speak up for them. It helps us to have the strength and authority to say no to others when we need to. Compassionate assertiveness is giving clear and direct messages while also being open to critical feedback from others without responding defensively. Compassionate assertiveness is a skill that takes some practice. We will learn about and practice this skill today.

Introduction to Compassionate Assertiveness

When we are compassionately assertive, we first try to notice what is happening inside us. Then, rather than attacking others, we can make a clear request for what we need. Automatic and impulsive responses can to lead us to attacks.

For example, if someone criticizes you, you might say, "Well, screw you! I hate it when you criticize me. You know that you're not the easiest person to get along with either, right? You have no right to criticize me. You're way worse than I am!"

On the other hand, when we act with compassionate assertiveness, we are careful not to have an automatic response. You may feel yourself getting upset but try to remember the skills we have learned to activate our soothing system. For instance, if you are in the red circle, you may find it helpful to focus on your breathing. It can also be helpful to consider why we are feeling what we are feeling and what the other person might be feeling. We then want to commit to act in a way that does not intentionally cause harm while also not being submissive. So to act with compassionate assertiveness, we want to (1) use our skills to activate the soothing system, (2) be thoughtful about our emotions and what the other person is feeling, and (3) commit to a compassionate response. These steps will help us have compassionate assertiveness.

A compassionately assertive response to criticism would be more along the lines of "When I hear that, it really hurts me. I get upset because I think you don't care."

With a compassionately assertive response, you begin by describing what's happening inside of you (it really hurts) rather than attacking. Depending on the criticism, you might own your own behavior by saying something like "I can see my behavior has irritated or upset you. That was not my intention, so I'm sorry." This response is a good example of being thoughtful about our emotions and what the other person is feeling.

Keep in mind that your anger desire is to say something mean or hurt back. When you are angry, you want to force the other person to do what you want. While this may work sometimes, such reactions often have unintended consequences. The assertive self wants to clarify your personal experience without trying to get someone to feel fear, guilt, or some other unpleasant emotion.

When we are assertive, we pay significant attention to our facial expressions and our voice tones. Both facial expressions and voice tones can be quite threatening to others when left unchecked. Being aware of them is another way to be thoughtful about what the other person is feeling and responding compassionately.

When we are assertive, we show our willingness to listen to the other person and communicate with the intent of understanding them. As we do this, we try to come to a compromise that works for both.

The goal of assertiveness is to take the heat out of the conflict. Because it's the heat, rather than the issue, that often causes the problem.

Assertiveness involves many components. Let's take a look at Handout 10.1 to see some examples of what assertiveness is and what it allows us to do.

Give time to review **Handout 10.1**. Process reactions. Add any additions the group comes up with to the list.

> *So, we can see there's a lot more to assertiveness than simply dealing with conflicts. Assertiveness is a confident desire to be clear about how we feel. Assertiveness is about clearly communicating our desires while being committed to being helpful and supportive of others. Assertive is not being selfish! Being assertive also means that we are prepared for reasonable compromise.*

Process.

> *All right, let's approach a part of compassionate assertiveness that may be a bit trickier. How can we be compassionately assertive to others that we don't particularly like? What happens in our minds and bodies when we think about people that we don't like? How can we be compassionately assertive without being aggressive or submissive?*

Process. It may be helpful to share one of your own examples here if the group struggles with this. Write the responses on the whiteboard. Validate wisdom the group shares and link answers given to the three-circle model (ways in which anger or anxiety patterns can take control). Explore any fears and resistances to assertiveness.

> *It's very important to remember that compassionate assertiveness takes time and practice to develop—just like the other skills we've talked about so far. It takes time to be aware of and practice communicating assertively with others. There may also be some difficulties that come with assertiveness. For example, not everyone responds well to assertiveness. We might become worried about others not liking us if we are assertive. We may even begin to not like ourselves if we set boundaries and view ourselves as not being able to do "everything."*

Understanding What Assertiveness Is (and Is Not)

Materials: Handout 10.1

> *Let's look more into parts of assertiveness that may be difficult. Look at Handout 10.1. For a moment, please think about a conflict that you've had with another person. As always, nothing too major. Just something that was mildly distressing. What did you come up with?*

Write the participants' generated conflicts on the whiteboard or process as a group. Clarify what assertiveness is depending on misinterpretations.

Now, look at Handout 10.1 and underline the components of compassionate assertiveness that you struggled with during your conflict. With an open mind and curiosity (no judgment), why do you think you struggle with that particular piece?

Remind participants that it is easy to get lost in the idea that assertiveness is only about conflict when, in fact, conflict is only one component.

Sometimes it's easier to understand something when you understand what that it is not. Here are a few examples of what assertiveness is not*:*

- *Minimizing your own values and needs*
- *Being overly focused on pleasing others to avoid rejection*
- *Letting others take responsibility rather than stepping up*
- *Not giving honest feedback to other people to avoid conflict*
- *Not making requests of others to help you or provide you with what you would like*
- *Acting out of impulsive emotion rather than compassionate wisdom*

Let's try to apply this. Let's take a minute and think about various responses to the following situations:

You just bought something from a store and realize it is broken and needs to be returned. The clerk at the return counter is questioning whether they can actually take it back. Try to notice what happens in the body when you are faced with a conflict. This would be a time to switch into slower breathing, grounding, and focusing on your compassionate intention (activate the soothing system). Think about your emotions, how they might affect the clerk, and how the clerk might be feeling. Think of different responses you might have. How would you respond to this clerk using:

- *An aggressive response*
- *A passive or submissive response*
- *A compassionately assertive response*

Pair up and share your responses with your partner.

Let's try another. Imagine you are feeling a bit lonely, and you want to ask a friend to spend time with you. Remember to include how you might need to activate the soothing system, and remember your and the friend's emotions. Pair up and share your responses:

- *An aggressive or demanding request*
- *A passive or submissive request*
- *Compassionately assertive request*

Next, imagine you're in a group and your group members are making suggestions that go counter to the suggestions that you have already made. Apply the same steps. Share with your partner:

- *An aggressive "I know best, and there is no way I am wrong" response*
- *A passive waiting-to-be-asked-your-opinion response*
- *Compassionately assertive response*

Process and highlight that a compassionately assertive communication style stays friendly while at the same time firm and respectful. This way of communicating is helpful and clear.

Expressing Appreciation for Each Other (Optional)

This optional section is provided at the end of the module. It may be helpful for those who struggle to express appreciation for others.

Asking for What We Need with Compassionate Assertiveness

Materials: Handout 10.2
Handout 10.3

Now, let's look at Handout 10.2 and start by thinking about a situation in which you may normally avoid asking for what you need. This may be a recent situation where you have been asked to do something and you said yes—but in fact you wanted to say no. This may be a situation where you were not assertive but maybe submissive/passive or maybe even aggressive. When you have something in mind, begin by (1) activating your compassionate self. Slow your breathing and your mind and bring to mind your compassionate self. (Pause.)

Again, bring the moment to mind that you thought about. (2) Think of how difficult it was for you to be assertive and ask for what you need. (3) Then think of things from your compassionate-self perspective:

What are your feelings in this situation?

What are your needs in this situation?

From your compassionate-self perspective, what would you like to say? What would you like to do?

Process. Highlight differences between participants' particular communication style (e.g., passive, aggressive, anxious, etc.) and their compassionate self. This is not their fault: we have learned various communication patterns from our environment. It is very likely that certain communication styles have "seemed to work" and have been beneficial at some point in time. It may not be the case now, though.

Did the compassionate self help? How?

Process. Maybe the assertive compassionate self is more helpful.

Imagine the potential benefits of expressing your needs and getting what you want/need. Maybe visualize yourself after five years of practicing this kind of communication. What do you see as you imagine this? Is this hard to imagine?

Process.

Note for the Group Leader

Assertiveness may be an especially difficult skill for one with severe mental illness to practice or acquire. Assess resistance here, notice how hard it appears to be for all or some to image a future being assertive. Explore what gets in the way if this is challenging. Discuss how diagnoses (especially schizophrenic spectrum diagnoses) can make it hard to be assertive especially in an inpatient setting. Explore additional ways assertiveness might be challenging (e.g., addiction, family of origin, personality, gender, race, etc.). Validate and circle back to the benefits of assertiveness despite challenges.

You have a doctor's appointment tomorrow that you have been waiting for a while. Your friend calls you and wants you to help her with some easy to do chore at the same time tomorrow. You want to say no because the appointment is very important to you. Try to notice what happens in the body when you think about saying no. This would be a time to switch into slower breathing, grounding, and focusing on your compassionate intention (activate the soothing system). Think about how difficult it will be to say no to your friend. Think of what your compassionate self would tell you. How would you respond to your friend using compassionate assertiveness? Remember those steps. Would you use:

- *An aggressive response*
- *A passive or submissive response*
- *A compassionately assertive response*

Take a moment to write your responses down in Handout 10.3. Write down what the outcome might be with each approach. For example, how might you feel if you respond each way? How might your friend react is your respond each way?

Pair up and share your responses with your partner.

Responding to a Criticism with Compassionate Assertiveness (Optional)

This optional section is provided at the end of the module. This exercise may be helpful for group members who struggle to apply assertiveness due to self-criticism.

Reviewing Compassion Process

Reminder

You can review the Jordan content from previous modules as needed, or you can go straight to the example from this module. Often a review is not necessary when time is short, and briefly apply the skills learned that day to Jordan's situation is sufficient.

Optional Review

Module 1: Dayroom fight, level drop, anger/anxiety, thinking loops; trick brain, "not my fault but my responsibility"
Module 2: Jordan's red circle scenario (anger); three circles, soothing rhythm-breathing
Module 3: Jordan's rumination on level drop, lingering anger; attention (flashlight), soothing rhythm-breathing
Module 4: Jordan's continuing threat mode; feelings safe through secure place/compassionate other imagery
Module 5: Jordan intentionally shifts to compassion; self-compassion in action (wisdom, strength, commitment)

Module 6: Jordan's dayroom situation produces multiple emotions; compassionate self understands and balances emotions
Module 7: Jordan's self-criticism; understanding inner critic and turning to growth through compassion
Module 8: Jordan's shame from yelling at the staff; compassion to switch to guilt and remedy situation
Module 9: A concrete exercise for Jordan's compassionate self; compassionate letter-writing

Let's apply what we learned today to Jordan. Jordan tries to use compassionate assertiveness to improve his situation and communicate his needs. Jordan was really angry when his level was dropped, so he asks if he can call his friend. When asked why, he explains that his level was dropped and he is distressed about it, so he would like to talk to his friend. Here, Jordan is being assertive and expressing his needs. The staff understand and allow him to call his friend.

Right then, another patient, Taylor, asks to use the phone. Jordan figures that if Taylor needs the phone more than him, then he will think of letting him go first. Here, Jordan is being compassionate. So, Jordan asks Taylor why he needs the phone. Taylor explains that he already called his sister three times today but wants to call her again. Jordan acknowledges Taylor but informs him that he needs to call his friend first. He tells Taylor the same thing he told the staff—his level was dropped, and he really needs to talk to his friend. Taylor responds by pressuring Jordan to let him use the phone first. But Jordan stays calm and tells him, "I'm going through a really hard time right now, and it makes me feel like you don't care when you pressure me to let you use the phone first." By saying this, Jordan makes his emotions clear. Taylor understands, and Jordan is able to call his friend. As Jordan asked to call his friend and said no to letting Taylor go first, he was showing compassionate assertiveness. Jordan was willing to listen to others, but he was clear about his needs and feelings.

Between-Session Practice

Generating Compassion

As we prepare to develop our compassionate intention:

1. *Sit with a straight back. Keep your head upright and your shoulders in line with your hips. Place your feet flat on the floor.*
2. *Lift your shoulders up and slightly backward.*

3. *Find a comfortable position for your hands that will not be distracting to you.*
4. *Breathe into your belly rather than your chest.*
5. *Bring a friendly facial expression to your body posture.*
6. *Gently fix your gaze on a single spot on the floor or close your eyes if you feel comfortable.*

Now bring your attention to your breathing. Connect with your soothing rhythm-breathing, with your mind slowing down and body slowing down. Pay attention to your mind and body as you do this. Gradually get that sense of grounding with a sense of stilling and slowing but also with an alert mind. Notice yourself becoming more grounded. (Longer pause.)

Now start connecting with your inner compassionate mind. Remember the wisdom that you have been developing in the course so far. We all have tricky brains and certain life experiences that have shaped how our minds and bodies work. Even though our tricky brains and life experiences have affected who we are, we also have minds that can learn how to change and make choices. We are developing the strength and commitment to help ourselves and others deal with the difficulties of life.

Acknowledge your courage and willingness to embark on this journey of learning, regardless of current circumstances. Acknowledge yourself for being open to learning and growing. You have the courage to stretch your boundaries, even if it's difficult, tricky, and scary. It's scary for everyone. Acknowledge yourself for being here exactly as you are.

You might do this in the form of a wish, something like:

- *May I accept myself in this moment of learning exactly as I am.*
- *May I give myself all the support and all the kindness I need in this moment.*
- *May I accept all of my difficulties and doubts with compassion.*
- *May I give myself all the compassion I need in this moment.*

Gently ask yourself, "[Name], what do you want to take home from today's session?" Think about what lessons from this session will be the most helpful to you. Listen to whatever arises with curiosity.

Remember why we are in this group: to work on ways to be helpful to ourselves, to support others as best we can on their journey, and to be open to the helpfulness of others. Silently repeat these three flows of compassion back to yourself.

As we bring this practice of developing our compassionate intention to a close, connect with your body again. Feel your body in the chair in this moment. Slowly start to come back into the room, and open your eyes when you are ready.

Components of Compassionate Assertiveness

ASSERTIVENESS

- is confidence
- is respect for yourself and others
- is the ability to express concerns and needs
- is recognizing where another person is coming from
- is NOT allowing threat emotions to take over
- allows us to acknowledge our mistakes without feeling critical
- allows us to disagree with others without feeling attacked or shamed
- allows us to ask for and accept help
- is being genuinely empathetic to ourselves and others
- takes practice
- ______________________________
- ______________________________
- ______________________________

Handout 10.1 Components of Compassionate Assertiveness

Reflections of the Compassionate-Self

- **Think** of a situation when you would normally avoid asking for what your need.

___

- **Activate** your compassionate-self.
  - Move into your compassion body posture
  - slow your breathing, thinking "mind slowing down" and "body slowing down"

From your compassionate-self perspective…

- **What are my feelings in this situation?**

___

___

- **What are my needs in this situation?**

___

___

- **From my compassionate-self perspective, what would I like to say and do?**

___

___

Remember the motivation of the compassionate-self: to be understanding, respectful and helpful to ourselves while listening and trying to meet the needs of others.

Handout 10.2 Reflections of the Compassionate Self

Exploring Ways to Respond to Others

Example: You have a doctor appointment tomorrow. Your friend calls you and wants you to help her with some easy-to-do chore at the same time tomorrow. You want to say "no" because this appointment is very important.

An aggressive response: ____ ____ **Outcome:**____________________________________
A passive or submissive response: ____ ____ **Outcome:**____________________________________
A compassionately assertive response: ____ ____ **Outcome:**____________________________________

Handout 10.3 Exploring Ways to Respond to Others

Optional Material

Understanding What Assertiveness Is (and Is Not): Expressing Appreciation for Each Other

Please sit in pairs with your chairs facing one another. Let's go ahead and (1) engage our compassionate self once again. Slow your breathing and your mind. Now, bring your compassionate self to mind. (Pause.)

Taking turns, one of you will express something about your partner that you appreciate using a friendly voice tone and compassionate facial expression. We'll then switch. Please know that this may be hard to do—that's okay. Just (2) notice your resistances and try to access your compassionate self as the compassionate self can help us both in giving and receiving appreciation.

How was that? What did you notice? Was it easier to receive or to give? What was hard?

Process. Pay particular attention to the resistances. Highlight the fact that compliments/expressions of appreciation from others can "conflict" with what our critical self may feel about us.

So, the way to use compassionate assertiveness to express appreciation for others is to first to engage your compassionate self and notice your resistance and the struggles you might have when accepting or giving appreciative comments.

Asking for What We Need with Compassionate Assertiveness: Responding to a Criticism with Compassionate Assertiveness

Short Guidance

Let's talk for a minute about some different forms of criticism. For this exercise, we're going to focus on moments when others are critical toward us, which is different from when we are critical toward ourselves. How do you notice that others are critical of you?

Process and write the responses on the board. Add the following if these are not offered by participants.

Here are some other criticisms that are fairly common:

- *Accurate criticism: "You didn't do [insert task] the way I showed you"*

- *Silent criticism: Rolling of eyes, tapping fingers, impatiently, etc.*
- *Hidden criticism: "Black clothes look good on you—they're so slimming."*
- *Nasty criticism: "You are stupid!"*
- *Explicit criticism: "I don't like you."*

Let's take a look at Handout 10.3. How might our "multiple emotions" react to these criticisms? How do they react? How does our compassionate self-react to criticism? How is our compassionate self assertive? How is this helpful?

Let's try to apply this. Let's take a minute and think about various responses to the following situations:

You are at work and you spent a lot of time cleaning one of the appliances like you were asked. Your boss comes in and points out several areas that are obviously not clean, describes how he wanted it done, and points out that he told you that before. He doesn't point out all the things you did right. Try to notice what happens in the body when you are faced with accurate, and unpleasant, criticism. This would be a time to switch into slower breathing, grounding, and focusing on your compassionate intention (activate the soothing system). Think about your emotions, how your emotions might affect your boss, and how your boss might be feeling. Think of different responses you might have. How would you respond to your boss using:

✓ *An aggressive response*
✓ *A passive or submissive response*
✓ *A compassionately assertive response*

Pair up and share your responses with your partner.

Let's try another. Imagine you tell your roommate about your experience at work. They roll their eyes at you and shake their head. Remember to include how you might need to activate the soothing system, and remember your and the friend's emotions. Pair up and share your responses:

- *An aggressive or demanding request*
- *A passive or submissive request*
- *Compassionately assertive request*

Next, imagine you are wearing a new shirt. Someone says, "Oh, a new shirt! That is an interesting color." Apply the same steps. Share with your partner:

- *An aggressive "I know best, and there is no way I am wrong" response*

- *A passive waiting-to-be-asked-your-opinion response*
- *Compassionately assertive response*

Next, imagine you're are trying to get on the bus and realize you don't have exact change. You find it, but it slows down the line. Someone says, "Be ready next time you idiot." Apply the same steps. Share with your partner:

- *An aggressive "I know best and there is no way I am wrong" response*
- *A passive waiting-to-be-asked-your-opinion response*
- *Compassionately assertive response*

Next, imagine you are at a party and just met someone that hasn't been in your group of friends before. After a few minutes of talking, the person says, "I don't think I really like you." Apply the same steps. Share with your partner:

- *An aggressive "I know best, and there is no way I am wrong" response*
- *A passive waiting-to-be-asked-your-opinion response*
- *Compassionately assertive response*

Process and highlight that a compassionately assertive communication style stays friendly while at the same time firm and respectful. This way of communicating is helpful and clear.

Process. Reintroduce **Handout 10.1** as a way to help them remember and reflect on what assertiveness is, if needed to overcome criticism.

Module 11

Forgiveness

REMEMBER: Do not sacrifice the moment for the manual. Be sure to assess and attend to diversity in terms of demographic as well as diagnoses within the group. Be aware of reasons for referral; this will inform fears, blocks, and resistances toward treatment that may arise throughout the duration of the group. This initial awareness of patient presentation and circumstance will allow the group leader(s) to better facilitate cohesion and participation.

Aims:

- Introduce group members to the flow of compassion for others.
- Explore how other people who suffer can influence us and how others' suffering can impact the way we feel in our body and how we respond.
- Explore ways to be compassionate to others.
- Understand fears, blocks, and resistances toward compassion for others.
- Discuss the concept of forgiveness.
- Explore how one might feel that others or themselves deserve suffering as a potential block to forgiveness.
- Explore ways to develop compassion for people we don't like.

Welcome, Soft Landing, and Personal Practice

Welcome participants to the group.

Short Guidance Soft Landing

> *To start today, like usual, we are going to do a soft landing and consciously experience the intention to develop our compassionate mind and pattern.*

DOI: 10.4324/9781003607557-11

Get comfortable in your chairs, feet flat on the floor, sitting straight, shoulders back and chest open. If you are comfortable, gently close your eyes or, if you prefer, just direct your gaze downward.

Now slow down your breathing a little and settle into your mind and body. Remember your body posture, facial expression, and voice tone.

Always respect the process, prepare your body, and open your heart.

Now, let's focus on soothing rhythm-breathing I will count you into this by saying: "In, 2, 3; out, 2, 3. In, 2, 3, 4; out 2, 3, 4. In, 2, 3, 4, 5; out, 2, 3, 4, 5." (Count about 1 second apart—remember to keep your counting steady)

As you develop your rhythm, notice and focus on the feeling of inner slowing with each out-breath. Gradually move toward that sense of grounding; a sense of stilling/slowing while maintaining an alert mind. Notice yourself becoming more grounded.

On each alternate out-breath say with a friendly supportive voice "Body slowing down" and then "Mind slowing down."

Tune into your inner compassion—attend to and remember the wisdom that you have been developing in the group so far. We all just find ourselves here with a very tricky brain and certain life experiences that have shaped how our minds and bodies work. But we can learn how to change and make choices. We can develop the strength, authority, and commitment to help ourselves and others deal with life and inner difficulties.

As we are sitting here, we say in a friendly and committed way:

I am coming here today in order to:

- *Develop compassion for myself.* (Pause.)
- *Increase compassion for others.* (Pause.)
- *Be open to compassion from others.* (Pause.)

Now, I invite you to think of someone you care about. Bring this person to your mind as if he or she were standing here in front of you.

With this person in mind, try to send him or her the following compassionate wishes from all your heart:

- *May you be happy.*
- *May you be free of suffering.*
- *May you be healthy and strong.*
- *May you be able to live in this world peacefully, joyfully, with ease.*

Between-Session Practice Check-In

Check that group members were able to engage in between-session practice. Check in to see if any group members thought about or used and part of CFT outside of group. Help the group process their experience, both successes and resistances. You may decide to share a personal reflection on how you integrated ideas from the previous session into your own life.

Okay, now just start to let these thoughts and motivations go. Start to come back slowly into the room, noticing your bodies in the chair and feet on the ground. When you are ready, you can open your eyes.

Welcome [back] to Module 11.

Bridge and Forecast

You may want to draw the three flows of compassion on the whiteboard and remind the group members of how they connect, emphasizing the flow of compassion to others for this module.

In the last session we learned about compassionate assertiveness. We also talked about how compassion is not weak but requires a certain kind of courage. Today we're going to focus on the last flow of compassion—compassion for others. We're going to focus on when compassion for others is the most difficult: when we're having conflict with another. We'll also introduce a new way to think about forgiveness.

Introduction to Compassion for Others

Compassion for Others

We all find ourselves here in a short-lived way. Impermanence is the notion that everything comes into existence and goes out of existence, including us; nothing and no one lasts.

Nobody chooses their gender, ethnicity, or personality. We are all trying to do the best we can to manage pain and avoid suffering. We all have built-in desires, wants, and wishes. We also all have fears.

Process. Help group members think about the commonalities of humanity. Essentially, we are all in the same boat.

> *We all have a body and brain that's been built for us but not by us. So many things can hit us out of the blue. Suffering is one of those things that can kind of take us by surprise and suffering is all around us. Can you think of ways of how every human must deal with pain and suffering, how we are all the same regardless of our age, gender, mental illness, wealth, education, etc.?*
>
> *Think about your multiple emotions in relation to suffering. What are the typical emotions you feel when you see someone who is struggling, suffering, or depressed?*

Process. Help group members explore that we can have many different feelings related to suffering of others (anger, anxiety, sadness, etc.) and that this depends on context. Compassion to others required us to do something about these feelings.

> *Life is filled with moments of suffering. We can be moved by suffering and want to be helpful. That movement might involve different emotions, but what underpins those emotions is the motivation to be helpful. For a minute, think about your experience in this group. What experiences have you had with your desire to be compassionate and helpful to others in this group? What has made this easy? What has made this difficult?*

Process.

> *What about compassion for others outside of the group? How does relationships impact compassion? Are you able to be more compassionate with people you love? How do conflicts make compassion more difficult? Often, compassion and forgiveness are quite different for people we like than for people we don't like. How so?*

Defining Forgiveness

Materials: Handout 11.1

> *What is forgiveness?*

Process and write answers on the whiteboard. Make sure to include the benefits of forgiveness. Have participants turn to **Handout 11.1** for more ideas on what forgiveness is and is not.

Humans get into conflicts for a variety of reasons, and it is typical for us to have vengeance urges when there is conflict or we have been hurt. Forgiveness is about how we deal with vengeful feelings and desires. Forgiveness is how we cope with the conflicts in such a way that we are able to reduce our own suffering and increase compassion. We acknowledge the wrong that was done and figure out how to move past this wrong so we can heal the relationship. Forgiveness is a decision to let go of resentment or anger toward someone else. Forgiveness is not about condoning or liking being hurt or bullied. We are not *saying what the person did was okay. In meaningful relationships, forgiveness is part of developing closeness. So, the nature of the relationship is crucial to understanding forgiveness. Forgiveness is more likely if we are assertive and use conflict resolution skills. Again, forgiveness is not a submissive act.*

Dimensions of Forgiveness

When addressing forgiveness, it is important to consider some of the following questions:

- *Has somebody carelessly or intentionally been hurt? How serious is the act that caused the hurt?*
- *When harmful acts have occurred, such as a friend lying to us, then to what degree does the person causing the harm show guilt and remorse?*
- *How much do I like this person? How much do I dislike this person?*
- *Are there social pressures to forgive (which can actually interfere with genuine forgiveness)?*

Process the inhibitors and resistances to forgiving.

Motivation for Compassion for Others

All right, so now let's take a moment and slow down our breathing. Begin to access your inner compassionate self. (Allow a moment for this to occur.)

Remember that compassion for others reflects wisdom, strength, and commitment and does not mean that a person is acting against one's own interest. Now imagine for a moment that you encounter other people who may be suffering while you are at your compassionate best. How would you behave? What would your fears be?

Process. Write the responses on the whiteboard with particular attention paid to fears.

Compassion for others is difficult when we are involved in a conflict, when the other person or people are very different from us, or when others are doing things we don't agree with and go against our values. In moments like these, it is often helpful to think back to some of the basics of CFT and see how they apply to others and ourselves. For a moment, try to apply the statements I am about to read to others. More particularly, apply these things to others who are different from you or who you are in conflict with.

- *All humans are born with a tricky brain.* (Pause.)
- *We all suffer.* (Pause.)
- *All humans are born with genes we did not choose and then have experiences in an environment we did not choose.* (Pause.)
- *This is not our fault, but it is our responsibility.* (Pause.)

Process. If discussion unfolds around wrongdoing, guilt, or retaliation, explain that by engaging with other people compassionately, we give them the change to be at their compassionate best as well. Also, recognize that we cannot control the responses of others.

What did you notice?

Send Each Other Compassion Exercise (Optional)

This optional exercise, provided at the end of the module, involves having group members pair up and take turns giving and receiving compassion.

Deepening Empathy

Defining Empathy and Comparing to Sympathy

Being mindful of others helps us to become sensitive to our own feelings, to the feelings of others, and to tolerate when our feelings are distressing and unpleasant. How do you all define empathy?

Process and write answers on the whiteboard.

Empathy can be defined as the capacity to recognize feelings and understand what is happening within another person and why that might be so without judging them. The more we can understand the emotions of another, the easier it is for us to know how to best interact with them. Self-empathy is understanding that we have a tricky brain and understanding what we think and what we feel. How do you feel that sympathy and empathy are different?

Process.

Sympathy is our own emotional reaction(s) to another person's distress. It may be the same or different from the feelings of the other person. With affective empathy, we tune in to the other person's feelings, knowing they originate in them and not in us.

Affective Empathy Exercise (Optional)

This optional exercise, provided at the end of the module, involves group members getting into pairs and experiencing empathy for one another.

Compassion for Others in Difficult Situations and Forgiveness

Materials: Handout 11.2

Practicing Empathy

Have patients open to **Handout 11.2** so they can take notes. Break group members into pairs. If you believe the group you are working with would struggle to complete this activity with partners, complete the exercise as a group with a volunteer sharing an argument nonjudgmentally.

We're going to take a minute to practice perspective taking. That is, trying to understand the feelings, thoughts, needs, and intentions of others. Please take a minute and tell the person across from you, as non-judgmentally as possible, about an argument you had with a person you cared about.

For the one listening, please activate the compassionate self and listen mindfully and empathically. Try to recognize the potential feelings, thoughts, needs, and intentions of the person described by your partner.

Now reflect together. Think about and discuss the feelings, thoughts, needs, and intentions of the other person? (Give time for them to discuss and write down on the handout.)

Finally, share what your compassionate wishes might be for the other person. In other words, how would your compassionate self react to this person?

Okay, now let's switch roles. (Repeat the activity and give time to discuss.)

Process this exercise as a group.

Did your view of the argument change? If so, how? Did activating the compassionate self help you to "tune into" the other person's world?

Process this exercise in terms of forgiveness.

You can remind patients to review **Handout 11.1** to explain what forgiveness is and is not.

Let's take a minute to remember what forgiveness is and what forgiveness is not.

Were you able to feel forgiveness for the person you were in conflict with?

Forgiveness in Religion (Optional)

This optional content, provided at the end of the module, connects forgiveness to religious beliefs (specifically Christianity).

Compassion Letter (Optional)

This optional exercise, provided at the end of the module, involves writing a forgiveness letter to a person that the group member is willing to forgive, then reading the letter to a partner as if they were that person.

Forgiveness Exercise: A Person We Don't Like (Optional)

This optional exercise, provided at the end of the module, involves feeling benevolent wishes for someone that you do not like.

Reviewing Compassion Process

Reminder

You can review the Jordan content from previous modules as needed, or you can go straight to the example from this module. Often a review is not necessary when time is short, and briefly apply the skills learned that day to Jordan's situation is sufficient.

Optional Review

Module 1: Dayroom fight, level drop, anger/anxiety, thinking loops; trick brain, "not my fault but my responsibility"
Module 2: Jordan's red circle scenario (anger); three circles, soothing rhythm-breathing
Module 3: Jordan's rumination on level drop, lingering anger; attention (flashlight), soothing rhythm-breathing
Module 4: Jordan's continuing threat mode; feelings safe through secure place/compassionate other imagery
Module 5: Jordan intentionally shifts to compassion; self-compassion in action (wisdom, strength, commitment)
Module 6: Jordan's dayroom situation produces multiple emotions; compassionate self understands and balances emotions
Module 7: Jordan's self-criticism; understanding inner critic and turning to growth through compassion
Module 8: Jordan's shame from yelling at the staff; compassion to switch to guilt and remedy situation
Module 9: A concrete exercise for Jordan's compassionate self; compassionate letter-writing
Module 10: Jordan wants to call his friend, but someone else wants to use the phone; compassionate assertiveness

Now let's think of how to apply what we have been learning today to Jordan's situation. After getting in trouble, Jordan's automatic reaction was to be angry. He yelled at the staff for misunderstanding what happened. He blamed the new patient for getting him in trouble. But then Jordan remembers to try to have compassion for the new patient. He imagines what the new patient must be feeling. He remembers how hard it was to be a new patient at the hospital. Jordan imagines the new patient is probably feeling scared and overwhelmed. As Jordan thinks about how the new patient feels, he feels more compassion for him/her. This leads Jordan to compassionate forgiveness. Forgiveness does not mean that Jordan "forgets" that the new patient got him in trouble. Forgiveness means that Jordan lets go of his bitterness and desire for vengeance. He reminds himself that we all make mistakes. Jordan feels better and more soothed as he lets go of anger and forgives.

Between-Session Practice

Experiencing the Flows of Compassion

As we prepare to develop our compassionate intention:

- *Sit with a straight back. Keep your head upright and your shoulders in line with your hips. Place your feet flat on the floor.*
- *Lift your shoulders up and slightly backward.*
- *Find a comfortable position for your hands that will not be distracting to you.*
- *Breathe into your belly rather than your chest.*
- *Bring a friendly facial expression to your body posture.*
- *Gently fix your gaze on a single spot on the floor or close your eyes if you feel comfortable.*

Now bring your attention to your breathing. Connect with your soothing rhythm-breathing, with your mind slowing down and body slowing down. Pay attention to your mind and body as you do this. Gradually get that sense of grounding with a sense of stilling and slowing, but also with an alert mind. Notice yourself becoming more grounded. (Longer pause.)

Now start connecting with your inner compassionate mind. Remember the wisdom that you have been developing in the course so far. We all have tricky brains and certain life experiences that have shaped how our minds and bodies work. Even though our tricky brains and life experiences have affected who we are, we also have minds that can learn how to change and make choices. We are developing the strength and commitment to help ourselves and others deal with the difficulties of life.

Acknowledge your courage and willingness to embark on this journey of learning, regardless of current circumstances. Acknowledge yourself for being open to learning and growing. You have the courage to stretch your boundaries, even if it's difficult, tricky, and scary. It's scary for everyone. Acknowledge yourself for being here exactly as you are.

You might do this in the form of a wish, something like:

- *May I accept myself in this moment of learning exactly as I am.*
- *May I give myself all the support and all the kindness I need in this moment.*
- *May I accept all of my difficulties and doubts with compassion.*
- *May I give myself all the compassion I need in this moment.*

Gently ask yourself, "[Name], what do you want to take home from today's session?" Think about what lessons from this session will be the most helpful to you. Listen to whatever arises with curiosity.

Remember why we are in this group: to work on ways to be helpful to ourselves, to support others as best we can on their journey, and to be open to the helpfulness of others. Silently repeat these three flows of compassion back to yourself.

Pause

When could you use this exercise in your life? (Give time for responses.)

Process.

Optional Material

Keep in mind that any of these exercises can also be assigned as homework to be completed between groups.

Motivation for Compassion for Others: Send Each Other Compassion Exercise

Please go ahead and pair up with someone else and have your chairs face one another. For just a minute, slow down your breathing. Begin to access your inner compassionate self. (Allow a moment for this to occur.) *Taking turns, one of you must close your eyes and send your partner your wholehearted compassion for about one minute as I read some phrases. We'll then switch.*

- *Like everyone, the person across from you has suffered, is somehow suffering, and somehow will suffer.*
- *Like me, this person is struggling with a tricky brain and is here to develop the strength, the wisdom, and the authority to face what life brings and what our human nature brings.*
- *Like me, my partner will be helped by the support of others. I can send compassionate wishes.*
- *May you have the strength to accept and face what life brings.* (Pause.)
- *May you have the wisdom that pain is not our fault; it is not your fault.* (Pause.)
- *May you find the strength and courage to face difficulties and whatever you need to do to navigate this life at your compassionate best.* (Pause.)

Defining Forgiveness

IS:

- A way to move on from past hurt and pain.
- Allows us to let go of anger, resentment, and vengeful feelings.
- Part of developing closeness in a relationship.
- More likely to happen if we have good assertiveness.
- Something that we do for ourselves–not for others.
- ______________________________
- ______________________________
- ______________________________

IS NOT:

- Thinking the behavior of somebody else os okay or right..
- Staying close to someone who hurt you.
- Forgetting.
- Liking the person or needing to be friends with the person.
- A way to stop hurting.
- Easy
- ______________________________
- ______________________________
- ______________________________

Handout 11.1 Defining Forgiveness

Compassion for Others in Difficult Situations

Write down a situation when you were in conflict with another.
Next, activate your compassionate-self and respond to the following questions:
What might the other person have felt?
What might the other person have thought?
What might the needs of the other person have been?
What intentions might the other person have had?
What are your compassionate wishes for the other person?

Handout 11.2 Compassion for Others in Difficult Situations

Forgiveness Letter

Think of someone you would like to forgive. Remember, forgiveness is not always easy but a way we can heal and move on. In the space below, write a forgiveness letter to this person.

Handout 11.3 Forgiveness Letter

- *May you remember your commitment to try to be helpful where you can and not purposely or carelessly cause suffering to yourself or others.* (Pause.)

Switch and repeat the reading and then process. Pay attention to the resistances related to giving and receiving compassion. How was it giving compassion? How was it receiving?

Deepening Empathy: Affective Empathy Exercise

Again, affective empathy is the capacity to recognize the emotions that are being experienced by others. Let's break up into pairs again. Person A, close your eyes and think of something emotional, and as always, nothing that is too distressing. Person B, activate your compassionate self and from that position try to observe mindfully the slight changes in facial expression and body posture of your partner in this exercise. Notice how this feels. Try to empathize. (Allow about a minute.) *Now, let's go ahead and switch.* (Allow about a minute.)

Process. How did people feel when they tried to empathize and understand the emotions of the other? Where did their minds go? Highlight that focusing on the emotions of other people (for example, trying to detect their emotions and empathize with them) might help us suspend our ruminative internal focus. That is, empathizing with others can help to regulate negative emotions that might come from internal rumination.

Compassion for Others in Difficult Situations and Forgiveness: Forgiveness in Religion

There can be links to religious beliefs when we talk about forgiveness, particularly with Christianity. Sometimes, depending on what one believes, some can have a compulsion to forgive, or feel pressured to forgive. So, this can be a tricky boundary to establish. Remember, "forgive and forget" is not what we are going for here. If you are Christian, think about Jesus on the Crucifix as an example. In His moment of absolute agony, He did not hold vengeance. He did not forget what was happening. Rather he asked that they be forgiven and expressed that they did not know what they were doing. He suffered without acting out in vengeance.

Start by closing your eyes or looking down and feeling how you are sitting in your chair right now. Settle into your compassion posture with your back straight and shoulders in line with your hips while opening your diaphragm. Now, slow your breathing, and with each slower and deeper breath say, slowly and with a friendly tone, "Mind slowing down" and then "Body slowing down," alternating phrases on each out-breath—gradually getting that sense of grounding with a sense of stilling/slowing but also with an alert mind. Notice yourself becoming more grounded.

We become our compassionate self—with the wisdom, the authority, and the commitment of the compassionate self.

From the position of the compassionate self, write a "forgiveness letter" to a person you are willing to forgive. Again, as usual, please choose someone that is not too distressing. The motivation of this letter is to affirm your understanding of the situation, declare what needs have been hurt by the behavior of the other person, and at the same time express your willingness to move on and be free.

Give time for participants to write the letter.

Now, imagine that the person in front of you is the person that you are willing to forgive. Remember that the intention is to "set yourself free" of unnecessary anger that prevents you from living the life that you want to live.

From the compassionate-self position, please read your letter to the person in front of you, who is also in the compassionate-self position.

If you feel that you are not ready to say "I forgive you," you may start with something like "I have the intention to forgive you" or "I'm willing to work toward forgiving you because I want to be free and I'm willing to move on."

Allow time for each pair to read their letter to one another. Process. What was it like to read and to be read to? What resistances did people notice?

Compassion for Others in Difficult Situations and Forgiveness: Compassion Letter

Materials: Handout 11.3

We are doing to explore what it might be like to write a letter to someone you want to forgive. First, bring to mind a person who want to forgive. The more hurt someone has caused, the harder it is to forgive. For this exercise don't think of someone who is really hard to forgive.

Next, we will get in touch with our compassionate self. Start by closing your eyes or looking down and feeling how you are sitting in your chair right now. Settle into your compassion posture, with your back straight and shoulders in line with your hips, while opening your diaphragm. Now, slow your breathing, and with each slower and deeper breath, say, slowly and with a friendly tone, "Mind slowing down" and then "Body slowing down." Notice yourself becoming more grounded.

Have the group open to **Handout 11.3** to write their forgiveness letter.

From the position of the compassionate self, write a "forgiveness letter" to a person you are willing to forgive. Again, as usual, please choose someone that is not too distressing. The motivation of this letter is to explore the other person's situation, share your hurt by the behavior of the other person, and at the same time, express your willingness to move on and be free.

Give time for participants to write the letter.

If pairs work works for your group, continue to have group members pair up and read their letter to another, as if it was the person they are forgiving.

Now, imagine that the person in front of you is the person that you are willing to forgive. Remember that the intention is to "set yourself free" of unnecessary anger that prevents you from living the life that you want to live.

From the compassionate-self position, please read your letter to the person in front of you.

Allow time for each pair to read their letter to one another.

Process.

Compassion for Others in Difficult Situations and Forgiveness: Forgiveness Exercise: A Person We Don't Like

Once again, slow your breathing and access your compassionate-self posture.

Now, I would like you to bring to mind somebody that you do not like particularly well. Take a little bit of time in bringing this person to mind.

So, we now have this person we do not like, but we want to keep benevolent wishes for them. We wish that their life will turn out well for them and that at the end of their life they will die well, relatively quickly, painlessly, and surrounded by those who love them.

Given that we know people can die slowly and in pain, this is a benevolent wish not to suffer.

We are just holding these two different feelings in mind, one of disliking yet not holding ill-will and benevolent wishes in the sense of not wanting the other to suffer. We may never like them or wish to be their friend. We may never want to spend much time with them. Indeed, we may wish to never see them again, but we do not wish suffering upon them.

This is compassion.

Process.

Module 12

Envisioning a Compassionate Future

REMEMBER: **Do not sacrifice the moment for the manual.** Be sure to assess and attend to diversity in terms of demographic as well as diagnoses within the group. Be aware of reasons for referral; this will inform fears, blocks, and resistances toward treatment that may arise throughout the duration of the group. This initial awareness of patient presentation and circumstance will allow the group leader(s) to better facilitate cohesion and participation.

Aims:

- Revisit the journey that the group has been on.
- Start to focus on prevention and emergency strategies for future difficulties.
- Begin to envision what a compassionate future would involve.
- Finish with a gratitude exercise in which participants send compassionate wishes to one another.

Welcome, Soft Landing, and Personal Practice

Note for the Group Leader

This module is focused on how to continue to integrate CFT skills into daily life. It can be conceptualized as "relapse prevention." We have spent the last 11 modules learning how to increase compassionate views of ourselves and others, allowing us to move through life benefiting from compassion. In this module you will explore ways to continue to do that even after the group has ended.

Welcome participants to the last module.

DOI: 10.4324/9781003607557-12

Short Guidance Soft Landing

Welcome to our final module together. To start today, like usual, we are going to begin with a soft landing and consciously experience the intention to develop our compassionate mind and pattern.

So, get comfortable in your chairs. Place your feet flat on the floor. Sit straight, with your shoulders back and chest open. Find a comfortable position for your hands that will not be distracting to you. If you are comfortable, gently close your eyes. Or, if you prefer, just direct your gaze downward.

Now, slow your breathing down a little and breathe into your belly rather than your chest. Just settle your mind and body. Remember your body posture, facial expressions, and voice tone.

Always respect the process, prepare your body, and open your heart.

Now let's move into our soothing rhythm-breathing. As you develop your rhythm, notice and focus on the feeling of inner slowing with each out-breath. Gradually get that sense of grounding. Feel a sense of stilling and slowing while maintaining an alert mind. Again, notice yourself becoming more grounded.

With each slower and deeper breath say slowly and with a friendly tone, "Mind slowing down" and then "Body slowing down" each time you breathe out.

Tune into your inner compassion. Attend to and remember the wisdom that you have been developing in the group so far. We all just find ourselves here with a very tricky brain. We all find ourselves with certain life experiences. This brain and these experiences have shaped how our minds and bodies work. But we can learn how to change and make choices. We can develop the strength, authority, and commitment to help ourselves and others deal with life and inner difficulties.

As we are sitting here, we say in a friendly and committed way, I am coming here today in order to:

- *Develop compassion for myself.* (Pause.)
- *Increase compassion for others.* (Pause.)
- *Be open to compassion from others.* (Pause.)

Now, think of someone you care about. Bring this person to your mind as if he or she was standing here, right in front of you. While keeping this person in mind, try to send him or her the following compassionate wishes from all your heart:

- *May you be happy.* (Pause.)
- *May you be free of suffering.* (Pause.)

- *May you be healthy and strong.* (Pause.)
- *May you be able to live in this world peacefully, joyfully, with ease.* (Pause.)

> **Between-Session Practice Check-In**
>
> Check that group members were able to engage in between-session practice. Check in to see if any group members thought about or used and part of CFT outside of group. Help the group process their experience, both successes and resistances. You may decide to share a personal reflection on how you integrated ideas from the previous session into your own life.

Okay, now just starting to let this exercise go. Start to come back slowly into the room, noticing your bodies in the chair and your feet on the ground. When you are ready, you can open your eyes. Welcome to Module 12.

Bridge and Forecast

We have now spent some time cultivating our compassionate selves to help with grounding and putting our compassionate minds to work. In our last session, we explored the different dimensions of forgiveness. Today we are going to bring it all together and review what we have covered over the past 11 modules. We're also going to look at how we can continue to imagine and cultivate a compassionate future.

Prevention and Emergency Strategies

Materials: Handout 12.1

Direct participants to the **final module review sheet** to review over the past 11 modules.

Direct participants to **Handout 12.1**. Make sure pens are available. You can simply walk through this worksheet for this exercise or use the following paragraphs.

The purpose of this exercise is to reflect on the different exercises, strategies, and practices that you have all been learning over the past several weeks and to try to put them into place as possible prevention strategies. Remember that the definition of compassion includes not only alleviating suffering when it occurs, but also preventing suffering when we can. As we work through this worksheet, try to be mindful of which areas are easier and which are more challenging. For example, is it easier or harder to come up with ideas about how to incorporate compassion for oneself and for others or to receive compassion?

What situations might you need self-compassion the most? What are things you could do during these times to access self-compassion?

Process.

What situations might you need to give compassion to others? What are things you could do during these times to give compassion to others?

Process.

This writing activity can be done individually and then, if preferred, participants can pair off and talk about their experience. It can also be processed as a group. Validate intuitive wisdoms as they arise.

What situations might you need to receive compassion from others? What are things you could do during these times to receive compassion from others?

Process.

Here are some other questions that might be helpful to ask: Is it easier to come up with suggested actions for emergency than for prevention? Do I focus more on one particular "flow" for prevention or for emergency? What fears do I have about some of my preventative or emergency actions?

Process.

Envisioning a Compassionate Future (Final Practice)

Materials: Handout 12.2

Today, we will be imagining what a compassionate future looks like for us.

To begin, we will engage our compassionate body posture.

Sit with a straight back. Keep your head upright and your shoulders in line with your hips. Place your feet flat on the floor.

Lift your shoulders up and slightly backward.
Find a comfortable position for your hands that will not be distracting to you.
Breathe into your belly rather than your chest.
Bring a friendly facial expression to your body posture.
Gently fix your gaze on a single spot on the floor or close your eyes if you feel comfortable.

Give a period to allow group members to experience slowing and stilling.

Now, imagine that you will be your most compassionate self from now on. Being compassionate has become your greatest goal. You will experience many ups and downs as you pursue your goal. However, you will continue to move in a compassionate direction.

Imagine your most compassionate self in five years. Imagine that you have been strong, wise, and committed to compassionate living. You remember the fragility of being human and bravely engage with suffering.

Now, consider these questions:

- *What qualities will you have developed in five years?*
- *What will the circumstances of your life look like?*
- *What dreams or goals will you have accomplished?*
- *Notice any feelings or sensations that arise when thinking about life as your most compassionate self in five years.*

Next, take a moment to consider how you will have changed in ten years.

- *What qualities will you have developed?*
- *What will the circumstances of your life look like?*
- *What dreams or goals will you have accomplished?*
- *Notice any feelings or sensations that arise when thinking about life as your most compassionate self in ten years.*

Write or draw this future in Handout 12.2.

Process. As a group, reflect on this visualization. Encourage all group members to share. What were the resistances? What were the fears? What was difficult? Any surprises?

As we bring this practice to a close, connect with your body again. Feel your body in the chair in this moment. Slowly start to come back into the room, and open your eyes when you are ready.

Gratitude and Compassionate Wishes (Optional)

This optional section is provided at the end of the module. It involves having group members wiring a gratitude letter to themself from their compassionate self.

Reflection of Experience

This can be done as a group or in pairs then as a group.

> *We are now coming to a close of our time together in this CFT group. As part of the process of closing, we are now going to break into pairs and have an opportunity to reflect on our experiences. We will then come back as a group and share what we noticed.*
>
> *As you break into pairs, please consider the following:*
>
> - *What were your expectations and what did you learn?*
> - *What did you find difficult in the training?*
> - *What can help you to continue to practice?*

Process what was discussed as a group and consider writing some of the responses on the board. Consider the following: What stood out as most helpful? Any struggles, fears, blocks, or resistances? Did you find out anything new about yourself?

Talk with the group about continued practice options (e.g., follow up groups, workbooks, websites, etc.).

> *Is there a symbol or an object that expresses what has been valuable to you?*

Compassionate Wishes Circle (Optional)

This optional exercise, provided at the end of the module, involves sending compassionate wishes to one another.

Reviewing Compassion Process

> **Reminder**
>
> You can review the Jordan content from previous modules as needed, or you can go straight to the example from this module. Often a review is not necessary when time is short, and briefly apply the skills learned that day to Jordan's situation is sufficient.

Optional Review

Module 1: Dayroom fight, level drop, anger/anxiety, thinking loops; trick brain, "not my fault but my responsibility"
Module 2: Jordan's red circle scenario (anger); three circles, soothing rhythm-breathing
Module 3: Jordan's rumination on level drop, lingering anger; attention (flashlight), soothing rhythm-breathing
Module 4: Jordan's continuing threat mode; feelings safe through secure place/compassionate other imagery
Module 5: Jordan intentionally shifts to compassion; self-compassion in action (wisdom, strength, commitment)
Module 6: Jordan's dayroom situation produces multiple emotions; compassionate self understands and balances emotions
Module 7: Jordan's self-criticism; understanding inner critic and turning to growth through compassion
Module 8: Jordan's shame from yelling at the staff; compassion to switch to guilt and remedy situation
Module 9: A concrete exercise for Jordan's compassionate self; compassionate letter-writing
Module 10: Jordan wants to call his friend, but someone else wants to use the phone; compassionate assertiveness
Module 11: Jordan blames new patient for dayroom situation; forgiveness, understanding new patient, letting go of bitterness

Let's try to envision a compassionate future using what Jordan has learned. Jordan thinks of the wisdom he has. He knows that we were born with a tricky brain. He knows he has life experiences he didn't choose. Even though he didn't choose them, his brain and life experiences shape who he is. That isn't his fault. But it is his responsibility to do what he can with the life he has. He can continue to develop the strength and commitment to help himself and others deal with life and inner difficulties. Jordan commits to continue practicing compassion. He uses soothing rhythm-breathing to move into the green circle. He uses mindfulness and imagery to notice and balance his emotions. He uses exercises like compassionate letter-writing to further develop self-compassion As Jordan applies what he has learned he is on a path to a compassionate future.

Final process of group experience. Say goodbyes.

Prevention and Emergency Strategies

Self-Compassion	
In which situations will I need self-compassion the most? • ______ • ______ • ______ • ______	**What are things I can do during these times to access self-compassion?** • ______ • ______ • ______ • ______
Compassion for Others	
In which situations will I need to give compassion to others? • ______ • ______ • ______ • ______	**What are things I can do during these times to give compassion to others?** • ______ • ______ • ______ • ______
Compassion from Others	
In which situations will I need to receive compassion from others? • ______ • ______ • ______ • ______	**What are things I can do during these times to receive compassion from others?** • ______ • ______ • ______ • ______

Handout 12.1 Prevention and Emergency Strategies

Envisioning a Compassionate Future

Imagine your future as your most compassionate self. You will experience many ups and downs but you continue to practice compassion. What is your future self like? What does your life look like? What dreams or goals have you accomplished?

Write or draw this future below…

Handout 12.2 Envisioning a Compassionate Future

Optional Material

Envisioning a Compassionate Future: Gratitude and Compassionate Wishes

Thank you for the time and efforts that you have put into this group. We'd like you to take a moment and acknowledge the efforts you have made as well. Take a moment again to access your compassionate self. (Pause.)

From your compassionate self, write a letter to yourself to express gratitude for your efforts. This may be compassionate self from the future, or it may be the compassionate self that is here right now.

For example, you may start by saying:

- *"Dear [your name], you are at the end of this path, for now. I want to thank you because . . ."*
- *"You showed the quality of . . . and this is valuable and helpful because . . ."*
- *"During this group, you [the action/behavior], which was helpful because . . ."*

Process.

> **Note for the Group Leader**
>
> You may consider reading the poems "The Five Remembrances" or "Call Me by True Name," both by Thich Nhat Hanh.

Reflection of Experience: Compassionate Wishes Circle

Before we leave today, can we take a moment to be in touch with our compassionate self once more as we say goodbye to those who have been in this group? We'll each take a turn, say our name, and send good wishes to the person who just said their name. Some examples of good wishes that might be sent include:

- *May you go on flourishing.*
- *May you have all the compassion you need to navigate the ups and downs of life.*
- *May your compassion set you free and help you achieve all your deepest desires.*

- *May you feel safe, may you feel happy, may you be healthy, and may you live with ease.*
- *May you be compassionate with yourself whenever you need it the most.*
- *May you be at peace with all the parts of yourself. May you love and accept yourself completely from now on.*
- *May your compassion help others and set them free.*

Appendix A

References

Braehler, C., Gumley, A., Harper, J., Wallace, S., Norrie, J., & Gilbert, P. (2013a). Exploring change processes in compassion focused therapy in psychosis: Results of a feasibility randomized controlled trial. The British Journal of Clinical Psychology, 52(2), 199–214. https://doi.org/10.1111/bjc.12009

Braehler, C., Harper, J., & Gilbert, P. (2013b). Compassion focused group therapy for recovery after psychosis. In C. Steel (Ed.), CBT for Schizophrenia: Evidence-Based Interventions and Future Directions (pp. 235–266). Wiley Blackwell.

Cattani, K., Griner, D., Erekson, D. M., Burlingame, G. M., Beecher, M. E., & Alldredge, C. T. (2021). Compassion Focused Group Therapy for University Counseling.

Cuppage, J., Baird, K., Gibson, J., Booth, R., & Hevey, D. (2018). Compassion focused therapy: Exploring the effectiveness with a transdiagnostic group and potential processes of change. The British Journal of Clinical Psychology, 57(2), 240–254. https://doi.org/10.1111/bjc.12162

Gilbert, P. (2009). Introducing compassion-focused therapy. Advances in Psychiatric Treatment, 15(3), 199–208. https://doi.org/10.1192/apt.bp.107.005264

Gilbert, P. (2017). A brief outline of the evolutionary approach for compassion focused therapy. EC Psychology and Psychiatry, 3(6), 218–227.

Gilbert, P. (2019). Psychotherapy for the 21st century: An integrative, evolutionary, contextual, biopsychosocial approach. Psychology and Psychotherapy: Theory, Research and Practice, 92(2), 164–189.

Gilbert, P., & Simos, G. (2022). Compassion Focused Therapy: Clinical Practice and Applications. Routledge. https://doi.org/10.4324/9781003035879

Heriot-Maitland, C., & Longden, E. (2022). Relating to Voices Using Compassion Focused Therapy: A Self-Help Companion. Routledge. https://doi.org/10.1080/17522439.2023.2172602

Heriot-Maitland, C., Vidal, J. B., Ball, S., & Irons, C. (2014). A compassionate-focused therapy group approach for acute inpatients: Feasibility, initial pilot outcome data, and recommendations. The British Journal of Clinical Psychology, 53(1), 78–94. https://doi.org/10.1111/bjc.12040

Mamani, A. W. D., Gurak, K., & Suro, G. (2014). Serious mental illness. In F. T. L. Leong, L. Comas-Díaz, G. C. Nagayama Hall, V. C. McLoyd, & J. E. Trimble (Eds.), APA Handbook of Multicultural Psychology, Vol. 2. Applications and Training (pp. 345–359). American Psychological Association. https://doi.org/10.1037/14187-020

Millard, L. A., Wan, M. W., Smith, D. M., & Wittkowski, A. (2023). The effectiveness of compassion focused therapy with clinical populations: A systematic review and meta-analysis. Journal of Affective Disorders, 326, 168–192. https://doi.org/10.1016/j.jad.2023.01.010

Appendix B

Full Jordan Example

Jordan is a made-up patient meant to help group members apply what they have learned during the session to a realistic situation. Applications from previous sessions may be reviewed before the paragraph corresponding to the current module if deemed appropriate. However, often going straight to the paragraph for the module is sufficient, particularly when time is short. Group leaders may present Jordan as female by altering pronouns if seen as appropriate or beneficial for the group. The narrative may be altered to better reflect the structure of your particular treatment setting.

Module 1

We will be talking about a made-up person named Jordan. One day, Jordan was sitting out in the dayroom when a fight broke out between a new patient and another patient. With all the commotion, it was unclear who started the fight and who was involved once staff showed up. The new patient blamed Jordan, as well as everyone else in the dayroom. The nurse decided everyone present would receive consequences and decided to drop everyone's level.

Let's apply what we have learned today to Jordan. Jordan has a tricky brain, just like everyone else. He was born with a brain and genes that he didn't choose. He was also born into circumstances he didn't choose. These circumstances have influenced who he has become. When Jordan's level was dropped, he became very angry and disappointed. These emotions are unpleasant and although Jordan didn't choose to feel them, he does. His mind starts to go in loops, and he repeatedly wonders how things could have been different. Jordan thinks, "I shouldn't have been in the dayroom. I should have stopped the fight from escalating. The staff are so unfair. I'll never get my level up. I've been working so hard and I'm not getting anywhere." These loops make him feel worse, but his brain was built to do this. He did not choose it, and it is not his fault. However, Jordan still tries to take responsibility for his emotions and actions. Jordan reminds himself, "It's not my fault, but it is my responsibility." Jordan also remembers the definition of compassion: sensitivity to suffering and distress in self and others, with a commitment to try to alleviate and prevent it. He recognizes that having his level dropped is hard for him. Then he starts to use this wisdom that helps him feel better. This is compassion.

Module 2

Let's think of how to apply what we have learned today to Jordan's situation. When Jordan's level was dropped, he got angry. He is in the red circle, or the threat circle. While he is feeling this way, Jordan remembers that every emotion is important, and that anger serves a purpose. He does not want to completely get rid of threat emotions (like anger), because they are telling him something important. However, Jordan can appreciate his emotions without remaining in the red circle. One thing he can do to move out of the red circle is soothing rhythm-breathing. To start this, Jordan brings attention to his breathing. He can gradually slow his breathing and ground himself. This helps him feel calm and allows him to move from threat to soothing, into the green circle.

Module 3

Now let's think of how to apply what we have been learning today to Jordan's situation. A few days after the dayroom fight, Jordan still thinks about his level being dropped. His attention is stuck on the past. When his attention is on his level, he stays angry. This is because our attention affects our emotions. Jordan remembers that he can change his emotions by shifting his attention. He notices that when he is focused on his level, he gets angry. As he realizes this, he tries to shift his focus to his breathing. Jordan wants to be in the present moment rather than stuck in the past. As he shifts his attention, he starts to feel calmer and at peace. He uses his attention as a tool to notice and balance his emotions. Using your attention this way is an important part of mindfulness.

Module 4

Now let's apply what we have been learning is this module to Jordan's situation. After Jordan's level was dropped, he worries he will get in trouble again. He finds himself focusing on potential threats. Any reactions from others make Jordan more upset than usual. After recognizing his emotions and realizing these worries are keeping him in the red circle, Jordan wants to feel safe. He remembers that he can use imagery to access a safe place. Jordan can also use imagery to increase his feeling of compassion from others. Jordan may think of an ideal compassionate other who understands how he is feeling and provides comfort. Jordan knows that the images in his mind may not be clear, and that's okay. As he uses imagery, he feels safe and supported. As he feels safe, he no longer focuses on potential threats. This helps him move out of the red circle and into the green circle.

Module 5

Now let's apply what we have learned in this module to Jordan's situation. Like us, Jordan already has some understanding of what compassion is. He can use that understanding to purposefully be compassionate. He knows that compassion is sensitivity to suffering and distress in self and others, with a commitment to try to alleviate and prevent it. Jordan is sensitive to his own suffering. He understands that having his level dropped has been hard. He also wants to help himself feel better. This is self-compassion. His wisdom, strength, and commitment all help him feel self-compassion. He has the wisdom that his brain was built to feel anger and that this is not his fault. Even though he knows it is not his fault, he has been trying to take responsibility for his anger. Jordan has the strength to notice his emotions and try to ground himself through mindfulness. He uses these skills to access compassion and balance his emotions. Even though it's hard, Jordan is committed to helping himself feel better. Jordan uses wisdom, strength, and commitment to have compassion for himself and live more intentionally.

Module 6

Now let's apply what we have learned today to Jordan's situation. Jordan felt many emotions when his level was dropped. He was angry with the staff, sad to be farther from discharge, and anxious he might get into trouble again. These are all "red circle" emotions, or threat emotions. These emotions want him to do different things. His anger makes him want to yell at the staff. His sadness makes him want to cry. His anxiety makes him want to stay in his room. With all these emotions, Jordan can feel overwhelmed. Jordan can use the compassionate self to help deal with his emotions. The compassionate self helps him acknowledge that each of his emotions are important. Through compassion, Jordan can value what his emotions are telling him without letting them take control.

Module 7

Let's see how Jordan experienced the inner critic. When Jordan's level was dropped, he experienced self-critical thoughts. Jordan thinks about how he should have been able to show that the fight was not his fault. He thinks, "If I was better about explaining myself and proving that I didn't start the fight, I wouldn't have gotten in trouble. But because I am not good at communicating with others, I was blamed for something I didn't do. It's my fault. I'm so stupid." These self-critical thoughts are not helpful, and they make Jordan feel worse about himself. When Jordan listens to these thoughts, they add to feelings of anger, sadness, and other negative emotions. However, Jordan realizes that his inner critic is just trying to keep him safe and connected with others–it comes from his fear of being rejected. As Jordan pays attention to his inner critic, he also remembers his compassionate self. Self-compassion helps Jordan start to change his thoughts. He thinks, "It's too bad that I wasn't able to show the staff that the fight wasn't my fault. Maybe things would be better if I communicated better. But we all make mistakes. Next time, I'll see if I can stand up for myself more." Jordan sees how self-criticism and self-compassion are different. Compassion helps him learn from his mistakes without attacking himself. In other words, he is allowing himself to fail compassionately.

Module 8

Let's see how Jordan deals with shame. After finding out his level had been dropped, Jordan yelled at the staff. He blamed them for keeping him from discharging. After a while, Jordan feels embarrassed about losing his temper. He thinks, "Now the staff will think I'm immature for yelling. They won't like me anymore. What if the other patients heard and now think bad things about me too? That would be so embarrassing." Do you see how self-focused these thoughts are? Here, Jordan is feeling shame. He worries that others are thinking bad things about him. When he is feeling this way, Jordan can use compassion to shift from shame to guilt. With guilt, Jordan thinks, "I shouldn't have yelled at the staff. They are probably doing their best. We all make mistakes, and I should apologize." Guilt helps Jordan want to make amends. Although he still feels bad for losing his temper, he is less focused on what others think and more focused on improving the situation.

Module 9

Now let's think of how to apply what we have been learning today to Jordan's situation. As Jordan feels upset, he remembers that there are many ways to increase self-compassion. One method he tries is compassionate letter-writing. He writes about how difficult it has been having his level dropped. In his letter, he expresses compassion toward himself. He acknowledges his anger. He tells himself that it is normal to feel angry.

Then he reassures himself that everything will be okay. Jordan reads his letter when he feels angry about his level. It helps him feel compassion and love. It makes him feel understood. Jordan is taking responsibility for his well-being as he uses these skills.

Module 10

Let's apply what we learned today to Jordan. Jordan tries to use compassionate assertiveness to improve his situation and communicate his needs. Jordan was really angry when his level was dropped, so he asks if he can call his friend. When asked why, he explains that his level was dropped and he is distressed about it, so he would like to talk to his friend. Here, Jordan is being assertive and expressing his needs. The staff understand and allow him to call his friend.

Right then, another patient, Taylor, asks to use the phone. Jordan figures that if Taylor needs the phone more than him, then he will think of letting him go first. Here, Jordan is being compassionate. So, Jordan asks Taylor why he needs the phone. Taylor explains that he already called his sister three times today but wants to call her again. Jordan acknowledges Taylor but informs him that he needs to call his friend first. He tells Taylor the same thing he told staff—his level was dropped, and he really needs to talk to his friend. Taylor responds by pressuring Jordan to let him use the phone first. But Jordan stays calm and tells him, "I'm going through a really hard time right now, and it makes me feel like you don't care when you pressure me to let you use the phone first." By saying this, Jordan makes his emotions clear. Taylor understands, and Jordan is able to call his friend. As Jordan asked to call his friend and said no to letting Taylor go first, he was showing compassionate assertiveness. Jordan was willing to listen to others, but he was clear about his needs and feelings.

Module 11

Now let's think of how to apply what we have been learning today to Jordan's situation. After getting in trouble, Jordan's automatic reaction was to be angry. He yelled at the staff for misunderstanding what happened. He blamed the new patient for getting him in trouble. But then Jordan remembers to try to have compassion for the new patient. He imagines what the new patient must be feeling. He remembers how hard it was to be a new patient at the hospital. Jordan imagines the new patient is probably feeling scared and overwhelmed. As Jordan thinks about how the new patient feels, he feels more compassion for him/her. This leads Jordan to compassionate forgiveness. Forgiveness does not mean that Jordan "forgets" that the new patient got him in trouble. Forgiveness means that Jordan lets go of his bitterness and desire for vengeance. He reminds himself that we all make mistakes. Jordan feels better and more soothed as he lets go of anger and forgives.

Module 12

Let's try to envision a compassionate future using what Jordan has learned. Jordan thinks of the wisdom he has. He knows that we were born with a tricky brain. He knows he has life experiences he didn't choose. Even though he didn't choose them, his brain and life experiences shape who he is. That isn't his fault. But it is his responsibility to do what he can with the life he has. He can continue to develop the strength and commitment to help himself and others deal with life and inner difficulties. Jordan commits to continue practicing compassion. He uses soothing rhythm-breathing to move into the green circle. He uses mindfulness and imagery to notice and balance his emotions. He uses exercises like compassionate letter-writing to further develop self-compassion As Jordan applies what he has learned he is on a path to a compassionate

Index

Note: Page numbers in *italics* indicate a figure on the corresponding page.

FSC
www.fsc.org
MIX
Papier | Fördert gute Waldnutzung
FSC® C083411

Kolibri 360 GmbH
Ferdinand-Jühlke-Straße 7
99095 Erfurt, Deutschland
produktsicherheit@kolibri360.de